POSITIVE WAVES
*a history of Indianapolis Racers hockey
1974-1979*

Timothy Gassen

PCMP Press
Tucson, Arizona

PCMP PRESS
P.O. Box 121
Tucson, Arizona
85702 USA

www.purple-cactus.tv

Copyright © 2007, 2009, 2013 & 2018 by Timothy Gassen

The logo of the WHA Hall of Fame is a registered trademark, used with permission.

www.WHAhof.com
www.whaRACERS.com

All rights reserved. No part of this publication may be reproduced, stored in a retrieval system, or transmitted in any form or by any means electronic, mechanical, photocopy, recording, or otherwise without the prior written permission of the publisher.

ISBN 978-0-9797337-1-0

Manufactured in the United States of America

First Edition published September 2007 with the title "Red, White & Blues: a personal history of Indianapolis Racers hockey 1974-1979," in 2009 as an electronic revised Second Edition, and in 2013 as a revised paper Third Edition with this new "Positive Waves" title. This is the revised Fourth Edition.

Front Cover: Racers promo poster, 1977
Back Cover: Wayne Gretzky, 1978 (courtesy The Indianapolis Star)

DEDICATION

It would be easy to simply dedicate this book to my Racers SuperFan brethren, Dave and Billy Pickering, still and always of Indianapolis. But we three share an important experience with those from 23 other former World Hockey Association cities: we have all lost our teams. Only the Edmonton Oilers (and a renewed Winnipeg Jets) still fight on in the NHL, the last remnants of the rebel WHA. So this book is dedicated not only to the fans and players of Indianapolis, but to all of us who remember our WHA hockey heroes. We can continue to watch the Oilers & Jets, grateful that they carry our WHA dreams with them, a reminder of our brief but shining place in hockey history.

PREFACE

Let's set the record straight: Indianapolis is a good hockey town, and explaining that idea is one main motivation for this book. Another motivation is to correct misinformation that has been passed through the decades about the Indianapolis Racers, the World Hockey Association, and Wayne Gretzky's entrance into professional hockey. To date, I know of no other book concerning Indianapolis Racers hockey that contains extensive, authoritative, firsthand reporting. In this book I have combined years of my own recent journalistic research, interviews and reporting with recollections of my personal interaction with the Racers. I then have added exhaustive research of previously published sources to complete this firsthand and accurate documentation of the 1970s Indianapolis hockey era.

As you read this book, understand that factual information and quotes which are included without attribution are from firsthand reporting, my period eyewitness accounts, and recent interviews I conducted personally. Other factual sources, including newspapers, magazines and books are attributed specifically in the text or photographic captions. This detailed attribution within the text is unusual for a book, but I've seen several authors writing about this era who repeat others' reporting as their own — and this is another practice I hope to set straight here.

TABLE OF CONTENTS

PART ONE: The Indianapolis Racers history 1974-1979 7

16-page photo section 57-72

PART TWO: interviews

Ken Block (player) 73
Al Karlander (player) 81
Hugh Harris (player) 89
Jim Park (player) 95
Ed Mio (player) 98
Dave Pickering (SuperFan) 105
Bruce Boggess (fan) 108
Randy Greb (fan) 111

16-page photo section 113-128

PART THREE: franchise statistics

All-Time Franchise Records 129
All-Time Player Roster 131
Intraleague Records 133
1974-75 Season Results 134
1975-76 Season Results 136
1976-77 Season Results 138
1977-78 Season Results 140
1978-79 Season Results 142
Regular Season Scoring & Goaltending Details 143
Playoff Scoring & Goaltending Details 148
Racers Playoff Results & Gretzky Scoring Record 149
Racers Franchise Player Transactions 150

PART FOUR: new edition materials
The Blood of Gilles Marotte 151

19-page photo section 154-172

Acknowledgements & Sources 173
Photo Credits & About The Author 174
Index 175

AN INTRODUCTION

Bill Libby, then with The Hockey News, wrote a piece for the October 17, 1974 opening night Indianapolis Racers game program titled "Reminiscences of a Hoosier Hockey Fan." He recalled Indy's minor league hockey of the 1950s, and was excited to see major league hockey finally come to his hometown.

He ends his piece prophetically — as if writing to me through more than three decades, as I write this book.

"Some day maybe you will want to tell about your old days in Indianapolis before the new hockey team became a top team. If the ghosts of the good old days are gliding along the ice of this swiftest and most savage of sports it will not be long before they invest their descendants with championship spirit.

"But it is not the championships I remember," he continued. *"It is the games. It is the rooting for your hometown team and for players you cannot forget even if most people never knew them. I can't forget them even if I haven't enough space to name them all. It is enough for me that I remember them. I hope it is enough for them that someone remembers."*

Dear Indianapolis Racers players, coaches, fans and friends — ghosts now one and all — I remember you.

I, too, hope that is enough.

Timothy Gassen, 2007

I am delighted that the success of the first edition of this book led directly to the formation of the WHA Hall of Fame and more preservation of Indianapolis Racers hockey history. This revised edition includes updated information, an additional photo section and a new Racers feature story. Join with me as we spread even more "Positive Waves" about Indianapolis hockey.

Timothy Gassen, 2013

INCUBATION

His skates dug perfect ruts and the metal clicked an impatient metronome as he rocked back and forth, urging the puck to the ice. The face-off couldn't come fast enough for "Mr. Hockey" — Gordie Howe — there was hockey to be played.

The Indianapolis Racers were barely out of the womb — the November 19, 1974 game was only their eighth home date, early in their inaugural season. I was 13, and it was my first pro hockey game. Howe, playing alongside his sons Mark and Marty with the opposing Houston Aeros, made sure it was not my last. A decade earlier The Beatles' appearance on Ed Sullivan's TV show signaled the nation's 1960s music obsession — and that first home game injected me with the same fervor for hockey — Indianapolis Racers hockey.

Gordie Howe was 46 years old at the time, ancient by mortal athletic standards, but even a novice like me knew he was considered the most complete hockey player of any era. And early on I noticed that my hometown Racers would back off from Howe when he chased a puck into the corners. I could see that Howe was still fierce, determined and relentless, but I didn't know then his elbows' reputation. The Racers did. My admiration for his superior talent, and the struggle for the Racers to keep up, was a microcosm for the Indianapolis franchise throughout its existence: They were the ultimate pro hockey underdogs, and like all good dogs, they did have their occasional day.

So if it's possible to love an idea, a concept — a team — then I was quickly in teenage love with Indianapolis Racers hockey.

ACCENTUATE THE POSITIVE

The Racers were conceived on April 10, 1972 as just a sparkle in the eye of John Weissert of the Indiana Professional Sports Management group. He told local media that he was seeking a pro hockey franchise to take up residence in the new arena set to be built in downtown

Indianapolis, and the hunt was on. The newly ordained World Hockey Association was glad to comply, and awarded a franchise to the group on September 14, 1973.

There was no way to know then that the greatest hockey player of all time — and perhaps the second greatest as well — would both wear Racers uniforms, and that the team would be the high water mark for professional hockey in Indianapolis for decades to come.

The Racers nickname was culled from a public offering of 145 entries, but in all honesty there couldn't have been any other hockey team name in a city so synonymous with car racing. (It didn't hurt that Indy's American Basketball Association team was already named the Pacers, and was controlled by the same Racers ownership group.) The local Wilson-Davis Advertising Agency created the unique, swooshing Racers logo, which was made public on February 26, 1974.

It was just seven months until the beginning of the inaugural 1974-75 season. Now all the Racers needed was an actual, breathing team — and enough fans to come see them play.

Indianapolis in the early 1970s was in transition from corn-belt capital to major modern city. The population boom of the 1960s pushed the metropolitan area over the magic million person mark, and the city sought to finally join the company of other Midwest leaders such as Detroit and Chicago.

In America, the best way to promote a major-league city image is with major-league sports. But in the 1970s Indianapolis was still considered a "tweener" — somewhere in between the regional minor leagues in baseball and hockey that the city had already sampled, and the top-level National Basketball Association and National Hockey League that were only then just beginning to expand. The NBA and NHL had frozen out Indianapolis for decades, with no thaw in sight, so Indianapolis embraced the rival league ABA Pacers and WHA Racers instead.

The battles between the NHL and rival WHA — and their seemingly endless attempts to merge — would eventually decide Indianapolis' major league hockey fate. But before becoming embroiled in the league wars, the infant Indianapolis Racers needed to create an actual playing roster.

The first Racers player signed was goaltender Ed Dyck, on April 9, 1974, followed by head coach Gerry Moore in June, and Andy Brown and Nick Harbaruk at the end of July. (Significantly, Dyck, Brown and

Harbaruk all had previous NHL experience.) Training camp opened in Flint, Michigan on September 15. Great struggles began for the franchise immediately and continually — with no calendar dates needing to be reserved.

The first Racers game with a recorded score was a 3-3 exhibition tie with the Minnesota Fighting Saints on October 3, 1974 in Flint. The home opener — two weeks later in a sparkling brand new Market Square Arena where the final touches were literally still being applied to the building — was a 4-2 loss to the Michigan Stags before 12,837 curious fans.

The Racers were born into the upstart World Hockey Association's third year of existence, and the league had quickly become more competitive and professionally operated since its 1972 debut. That spelled additional grief for a new franchise like Indy. Expansion teams are easy meat for established clubs, but even by expansion standards the Racers endured a brutal first season. Their dead–last league finish was no surprise, but the statistics were numbing: all–time WHA marks for most losses (57), most home losses (26), fewest wins (18), and fewest points (39).

There were only two true highlights from this debut season: the quality home ice and the gritty play of goaltender Andy Brown.

The new 16,040 seat Market Square Arena, with its 150-foot dome, was a stunning venue by any standard. It was as impressive as any arena in the world, and arguably the finest new hockey venue in North America. The sightlines for hockey were impeccable from anywhere in the building — even the very top row, as I found out regularly.

Fan Randy Greb remembered in 2004 the moment almost three decades earlier when the Racers and their lair entranced him as a young boy.

> *"When we arrived at MSA something took place that changed me forever: We walked up the long stairs to the middle concourse and as I walked through a tunnel that led into the seating area, a cold breeze hit me in the face. When I looked down I saw the ice surface and I was mesmerized. The red and blue Racers logo looked so bold, emblazoned on the freshly resurfaced rink."*

MSA was an impressive arena, but it was the action on the ice, and the Indianapolis fans' curious reaction, that captured Greb.

> "With less than a minute left, the Racers were down 3–0, but broke into the offensive zone and took a shot — and as the puck went past the goaltender everything slowed down for me. I saw the puck go into the goal and the net puffed out as the puck hit it.
>
> "The crowd was on its feet and cheered until the game was over. It's hard to imagine that a city would react so jubilantly when a game was out of reach, but that describes Racers fans. This city took hockey under its wing and loved it to death."

Goaltender Andy Brown was the final pro goalie to play without a mask, and "valiant" is the only term that accurately describes his superhuman efforts between the pipes in that first season. Continually left naked by a porous defense, Brown worked furiously to keep his crease clear so he could at least see the pucks rocketing at his unprotected head.

In the Racers' second game, October 18 at Toronto, an indignant Brown threw the puck at the Toros' Frank Mahovlich upon the game's final buzzer, racking up more penalty minutes to go with the other minor and misconduct he had already collected in the match. "He's a hot-head. I know that," coach Gerry Moore told the Toronto Globe & Mail.

It's no surprise, then, that in 1974–75 Brown earned 75 minutes of penalties — a league record for a goaltender. He would slash, poke, trip and every combination of the above to try to clear the traffic in front of him. Countless miracle saves made Brown the Racer to watch in that first season, and he was Indianapolis' lone selection to the mid-season 1974-75 WHA All-Star Game. Despite all the losses over this year and the next, amazingly his career Racers goals-against average ended under four (at 3.94 goals per game).

There was no quit in Andy Brown — and that was the quality that would lead the Racers upward under their new coach for the bulk of the 1975–1976 season, Jacques Demers.

THE FRENCH CONNECTION

The franchise ownership merry-go-round started up almost immediately in Indianapolis. The initial investors were out by December 5, 1974 of that first season, replaced by Paul Deneau, who previously owned the majority interest in the WHA's Houston Aeros. Intimately familiar with the WHA and its unique business machinations, it also seemed good news that Deneau was not an absentee owner, living in nearby Dayton, Ohio.

Surprisingly, one of Deneau's first decisions was to retain coach Gerry Moore, who appeared to be out of step with his team as it barreled headlong into last place. Dour and gruff, Moore was handcuffed with a rotating roster of professional leftovers, and could not figure out how to make a palatable casserole that could score goals and win games.

Moore was on board for the start of season number two, but after a predictable 1-4 stumble out of the gate, the trigger was finally pulled and Moore was put out of the fans' misery.

In came Jacques Demers, already in the front office of the Racers. Timing is everything, and the personable Demers seemed ready for the mammoth opportunity/headache that fell in his lap. While Demers had assisted with the WHA's Chicago Cougars, he had no head coaching experience and was next to unknown in professional hockey circles. And while having no head coach at all seemed to the fans a better option than another year with Moore, perhaps the thought was that Demers was a better option than no head coach at all.

The French Canadian Demers never hid his ultimate dream: to one day coach the NHL Montreal Canadiens to the Stanley Cup. That goal seemed ludicrous in 1975, however, as he began to claw his way up the coaching ranks through the bottom of the WHA. (Amazingly, Demers eventually realized his Stanley Cup goal in 1993, in his first year with the Canadiens, and also coached a variety of other NHL teams in his long and winning career.)

Demers guided the Racers to their best franchise moments, all between 1975 and 1977, and became the friendly, enthusiastic and positive public face for the franchise. Continually lacking in offensive power, he was masterful at preaching and selling a teamwide defensive system. He had to: Indy would never own a year-end WHA top 10 scorer, and their year-end team leading scorers from 1975–77 were defensemen. Demers managed to squeeze every ounce of effort from the Racers' out–manned personnel and somehow push them toward the WHA elite.

Defenseman Ken Block played the most games as a Racer, a whopping 267 contests from the middle of the expansion year until the franchise's collapse four and a half years later. The departure of Moore was a breath of fresh air for Block, who would deservedly wear the captain's "C" on his jersey for most of his time in a Racers uniform.

"I really enjoyed it in Indianapolis," he said in 2006. "The best thing about it, when Jacques (Demers) took over, he really jelled the team together. Jacques really had no experience as a coach — quite frankly the very first practice was probably one of the most disorganized ones I've ever attended. The thing with Jacques, what his forte was, is that he knew players. And he knew how to put a team together and how to get the best out of players and he treated players very, very well."

Demers also thinned out the players who he thought did not embrace his team concept. Only three players from the December 1974 roster were still with the club as of February 1976, when the franchise started to find its winning legs. And of the 22 players who started the Racers' second year, a mere 12 were still in the lineup as the club headed into the late season playoff drive.

As with any coach, sometimes Demers needed to exert his authority over a talented individual for what he thought was the best interest of the entire roster. "I ended up going to Indianapolis for a couple seasons, and then I had a falling out with (coach) Jacques Demers, and I packed it in for good," forward Bobby Whitlock said in Murray Greig's excellent book "Big Bucks and Blue Pucks."

"My first year in Indy I led the Racers in scoring and the next season I was seventh in the league in points when Demers said he was sending me to the minors because I wasn't scoring enough goals," Whitlock said. "That pretty much ended it for me. The fun was gone from the game, and I knew Demers was going to be around a lot longer than I would be."

Racers forward Al Karlander observed in 2006, "Coming off as bad a year as it was (the first year), I think the first right move was getting rid of a lot of the 'problem' players, not necessarily the best players or the worst players, it was more the problem players that weren't there to win. Having Whitey (Stapleton) there added some real stability, and then bringing in younger players like Kim Clackson, you got the bookends. You got Whitey on one end and Kim Clackson on the other."

Pat Stapleton was a former star for the NHL Chicago Blackhawks, and from 1975-1977 his calming, authoritative presence became the backbone for the Racers' defensive style. "Whitey" was his common nickname, referring to his flowing golden locks, but fans also called him

"The General" because of his deliberate pace-setting command of the game. Stapleton would punctuate his arrival in Indianapolis with his selection to the 1976 WHA All-Star Game.

Kim Clackson, the baby-faced, steel-strong and tough-as-nails young rookie defenseman, became the battery-charger for the Racers. Always ready to meet any physical challenge, Clackson would help jump start the team's second-season playoff run with a now legendary mid-season thumping of the New England Whalers' Nick Fotiou.

"During warm-ups, first thing Clacker did, he skated down and went through the other team's zone, right through it, like 'You know what? This whole ice belongs to us and if you guys don't like it, I'm the one you're going to deal with.' Now you get a penalty for doing that. Clacker was a great kid," Karlander remembered.

POSITIVE WAVES

Demers was emotional and fiery, but under his reign the Racers had their most stable lineups. The developing cohesion of the squad — playing low-scoring, tough-hitting, penalty-kill-at-all-cost games — took real form in the second half of the 1975–76 season. It was hard to believe, as the Racers sat again in the basement of the standings, that something magical was about to happen in Indianapolis. After a long road trip, the team began to talk publicly about something that inspired them, something called "Positive Waves."

The phrase reportedly came from the 1970 Clint Eastwood film "Kelly's Heroes," where a decidedly unbelievable WWII hippie character believes that successful attitudes give off "positive waves." The "official" version of the story was that some of the players saw the movie on TV during a road trip, and began using the phrase. It soon became the Racers' battle cry for their playoff run of 1976 — and I collected as many souvenir "Positive Waves" buttons as I could for accumulated good luck.

Racers leader Hugh Harris, original architect of the "Positive Waves" campaign, remembered the birth of the idea a little differently. "Well, actually 'Positive Waves' all started off basically in a bar. We were sitting in the bar — do you remember Teddy Scharf? OK, well we were sitting in the bar one day and he had put some money up on the bar and I said to him, 'What if the bartender had kept your money as a tip, you know, like a $35 tip for a couple of drinks?' And he said that he would kill him, that he'd grab him and shake the life out of the guy. And that's where all that nonsense started, because I said, 'That's the same thing that the other teams are doing! They're taking the money right out of your pockets.'"

So Harris took his barroom philosophy and transferred it to the ice as positive motivation. "We didn't care at that time whether we got down one or two goals because I can remember times in New England that we were down three-nothing and would come back, and it was the only time I played on a professional team or any kind of a team where that would happen — usually you get down three-nothing and the game is over," Harris said. "We'd been down as much as five goals and come back and win the bloody game. Now don't ask me how it happened, but it happened. We'd just say, 'You'd better score another one, because we're coming.'"

"Positive Waves" was in full swing by the time young goaltender Jim Park was called up from the Mohawk Valley Comets of the North American Hockey League for the Racers' stretch run to the 1976 WHA playoffs. "That good defense was already there, and I remember such a positive atmosphere around the team," Park said in December 2004. "We had some real characters on the team — Hughie Harris was probably the biggest one — and he got those 'Positive Waves' going, and that's what it was all about in the dressing room getting ready for games.

"We believed that if we kept the puck out of the net and scored a couple, we would win. And we were doing it for each other, because we had to — it was the only way we were going to win. With that Racers team it was life and death to score goals, and every night it was a battle. It was a lot of fun and a lot of hard work. The great part is that gradually you start to believe and rely on that belief — and then see the success it brings."

Park saw where much of the credit for the team's dramatic turnaround belonged. "I think a lot of credit goes to Jacques (Demers). He was right on with the team aspect of pulling together and emphasizing hard work. He wouldn't come in and yell, but he'd sit you if he thought you weren't working hard, and he very much encouraged the veterans like Hughie and Kenny Block and 'Balty' (Bryon Baltimore) to take over the room and get everyone prepared. He was a smart young coach to let the veterans like Pat Stapleton run the room — he was a good communicator, and that approach became very successful."

Harris isn't so convinced that Demers' contribution was essential. "According to Jacques, if the team is winning, they're playing his system. If the team is losing, they're playing as individuals, you know what I'm saying? There really wasn't any system. He's a great guy, but I think he got way too much credit for what he really did."

Regardless of who did what or how they did it, by mid-season the Racers together were starting to make a move in the standings. They were starting to believe they could win, they were starting to show an uncommon resiliency and determination — and the city of Indianapolis was starting to go bonkers watching their efforts.

Block, who still lives in Indy, sees the Racers' "Positive Waves" era as the benchmark of his career. "It was special, I gotta tell you. It was the same for us as I think it was for the fans that embraced the team. It was fun. Some of my best experiences in my hockey career was having played here during that time."

THE SUPERFANS

By 1975, a group of intensely loyal teenagers who called themselves "The SuperFans" were firmly entrenched in the rafters of Market Square Arena, as far up and opposite of the player benches as possible. A huge banner would stretch above them that read "SuperFans," created by teenage brothers Dave and Billy Pickering. Dave was the older brother by a year, with wispy blond hair, a quick laugh and sly sense of humor. Billy was stockier, more athletic and strong as an ox. Together, they were tough, funny and complete hockey hounds. There wasn't a mean bone in their bodies, but the fire they felt for Racers hockey was matched only by my own.

But they weren't the only fans in the stratosphere — for a while there were also "The Rafter Rats." "They were two ex–Chicago Cougars (WHA) fans," remembered SuperFan founder Dave Pickering in 2004. "Since the Racers picked up quite a few Cougars players after that team folded (including fan favorite Pat Stapleton), they'd come to Indianapolis for weekend games, with a big green and gold banner at the top of Market Square Arena that said 'Rafter Rats.' They had a snare drum and they'd get the crowd to clap in rhythm, making noise and raising hell."

One of the Rafter Rats literally wore his split loyalty between the NHL and WHA on his back, the product of two hockey jerseys cut apart and stitched back together vertically right down the middle: One half was the jersey of the WHA Chicago Cougars, the other the NHL Chicago Blackhawks. Now the Racers stood in as the replacement WHA team for the Rafter Rats' departed Cougars.

The Rafter Rats eventually faded, but the SuperFans only got louder. They quickly took me under their wing and showed me the finer points of hockey arena noise making. Their main weapons of choice were rubberized seat cushions they would whack on the concrete stair at the top of the arena. "Thump! thump! thump!" — the boom reached every corner of the massive MSA. We'd whip the crowd into a syncopated call and response, spurring on our heroes, making as much noise as possible. The occasional bugle and snare drum were also employed, but the trusty cushions always got the job done. Being a SuperFan wasn't very hip or elegant, but it sure was fun.

We were also teenagers, so much silliness ensued. The Pickerings taught me not to take hockey too seriously — when all looks lost (as would be all too common with the Racers) sometimes it's best to just have a laugh. So sometimes we'd explain away a stupid penalty the Racers took by arguing with each other in awful French Canadian accents, somewhat in the style of the TV show "Saturday Night Live" and their "wild and crazy guys" foreign swinger characters. By today's standards this was not at all politically correct, but it was harmless fun. And in the rafters — at least until the playoffs and the 16,040-fan sellouts — there was no one to annoy with our puerile antics.

We actually had great respect for French Canadian players, since we knew in the 1970s that hockey could elevate no higher than the ultimate Francophones — Les Habitants — the Montreal Canadiens. So the Racers' own Rene LeClerc became our version of the Habs' Guy Lafleur. A wonderful skater with a nifty wrist shot, LeClerc was never seen by us without his trademark turtleneck sweater and feathered John Travolta hair. (In a fan club photo of LeClerc playing an off-season volleyball game during his Racers years, I swear he is wearing that same turtleneck!) He was dashing, talented, fast — and yes — he spoke with a French Canadian accent that made him seem like a movie star.

LeClerc was also passionate about the game. On one shift, on a penalty kill, he blindly attempted to clear the puck up through the center of the defensive zone — a hockey no-no. Predictably, the puck was intercepted and one-timed back with a blast into the Racers' net. LeClerc trembled in disgust at his own mistake, and I thought he might break his stick over his head. He went to the bench and apologized to his teammates. He cared about his team — he was a winner.

I find it intriguing that of all the beautiful goals that LeClerc scored for the Racers, it is this simple defensive mistake that I remember so clearly. I think that, as a teenager, it struck me that LeClerc held himself publicly responsible when something "wrong" happened. He pointed the finger at no one but himself — he was responsible, and he let his teammates know it. The Racers were one-down on the scoreboard, but at that moment I held great admiration for Rene LeClerc. He'd get that goal back — or die trying.

We would wait for our Racers heroes dutifully after each home game, as they would emerge from the locker room, wade through the adult admirers, to reach our programs and pens for autographs. They autographed our programs over and over again, game after game, with a wink of good-natured recognition.

One and all, they seemed to relish the opportunity to have fans, to be able to play major-league hockey, and to be asked to sign autographs. This era of WHA players seemed to be grounded in a basic humility that is absent from today's million-dollar rookies. Many of these 1970s players knew that simply by existing in the right few years they had a professional major-league opportunity that did not exist before and could vanish at any time.

These Racers had a quality that would seem ridiculous and sentimental by today's selfish, crass, "me-first" professional athletes: they were thankful.

"The Racers were like having our own local rock stars," SuperFan Billy Pickering said. "They'd come out of the locker room in funky, long fur coats, with platform shoes and big afros, and they were like movie stars.

"Then I'd head over to the other locker room, where Bobby Hull or Gordie Howe was holding court. For a teenage sports nut in Indianapolis, it didn't get much more exciting than that."

There were other teenage fans enraptured by the visiting hockey royalty, too. "I remember Bobby Hull and Gordie Howe were always so nice to fans in Indianapolis," fellow teenage fan Bruce Boggess remembered in 2004. "I waited outside the visitors' locker room once to have Bobby Hull sign a picture for me. When he finally came out, all smiles and talking with everyone, he was wearing a full-length fur coat. I can recall nudging my buddy and saying, 'That's a superstar.'"

So the SuperFans studied the game intently from our high perch, coming down from our hockey nest only for souvenirs, drinks and autographs. We became so immersed in how the Racers played that we could tell which player was on the ice merely by how he moved his shoulders — and this was from the top of the arena.

Rugged forward Al Karlander echoed many former Racers in his admiration for the Indy fans' devotion to their team. "I don't think, personally, in all my years of playing, I felt more a part of the fans — and I felt like the fans felt a part of the game — in any other team I'd played on or witnessed.

"It was the fans — if we lost, they felt the loss and if we won, they shared the win. I think we felt like we were sharing it with them. I think a lot of times players walk away and they're happy, you know the fans got a win, but we're the ones that earned it, and it's our win, not theirs. But there was energy that was coming over and above just the normal good fan support."

HEROES

We had our favorite players, and nothing was more intriguing to a teenage hockey fan than a talented goaltender. Andy Brown had been fun to watch, but he was near the end of a long career. Now the Racers had a new legitimate talent in 21-year-old Michel Dion.

During the Racers' rise of 1975–76, Dion endured a minor injury and spent a couple days in an Indianapolis hospital. My SuperFan buddies and I figured he'd like some company, so we snuck into the hospital, past the hospital nurse and found his room. Cracking the door open, I found a buxom blond sitting on his hospital bed, with a bottle of wine shared between them.

Billy and Dave wanted to know what I was peering at, and pushed the door open. Dion finally saw us, and mildly perplexed, said in his French-Canadian accent, "Hello boys. Come on in. Come on!" He was friendly (and a bit tipsy), and didn't know that we had never seen one of our heroes with a pretty girl on his lap before. He thanked us for coming by and we told him we hoped he was better soon. Dave, slyly, said to me in the hall on the way out that we didn't need to worry about him feeling better — he was doing just fine.

So, for a 14-year-old, this was a fine life lesson: your heroes are people too. And far from ruining our worship of the goaltender, we were now convinced that being a professional hockey player was the best job on earth — even when you're injured.

The romance of the pro player's life was transmitted to us by radio play-by-play man "Hockey Bob" Lamey. "Hockey Bob" made even the most pedestrian element of a game a prelude to excitement, and I spent countless nights on my bed, eyes closed, as I imagined the Racers speeding up and down the ice in some far away city. The action was sharp and clear as it rolled out of Lamey through my tiny AM radio speaker, and he inspired me to dream of becoming a hockey announcer myself — a goal I eventually accomplished.

After the "away" games I'd call Nat Humphreys, my DJ friend at the Racers' host radio station, WIBC. We'd discuss the game (off the air), and he'd feed me inside Racers info to share with the SuperFans. Those tidbits — trade rumors, NHL talk, injury updates — were worth hours of conversation for Billy, Dave and me at the next home game.

Lamey would go on to broadcast NBA Pacers basketball, NFL Colts football, and the Indy 500 — but he'll always be known in Indianapolis as "Hockey Bob."

"Hockey Bob was such a huge part of the Racers," veteran forward Al Karlander said. "As a player we all had known play-by-play guys, but not somebody that cared as much as Hockey Bob. He took more stats and spent more time with us than the GMs did on other teams. That WIBC radio station was so supportive — Indianapolis is a basketball community but we got a lot of great publicity and it was the buzz of the town that the Racers was the fun thing to do. It was fun to go down there, and it was fun to play."

I didn't realize it as a teenager, but not all professional teams were inhabited by such passionate, likeable characters. Now I know that all hockey players are influenced by a unique combination of three conflicting motivations: the desire to please themselves, the desire to please their front office, coaches and fans, and the desire to please their teammates. It is natural for many professionals to think "me first" when their careers are short and their pain and efforts hard. Money, attention, fame and status can overwhelm and destroy some players if they are shortsighted.

Other players respect the responsibility that teams put on their shoulders. Many players in the WHA, for instance, were grateful to certain coaches or GMs for the chance to prove themselves at a major league level, with increased pay, too. Cast off from other teams and other leagues, they took the opportunity of the World Hockey Association very seriously, and with personal pride.

The level of connection between fans and the Racers themselves was unusually strong, and I'm quite certain that the balance of a number of crucial games was tipped to the Racers' advantage by that positive energy. Some players are highly motivated to achieve great things for their fans — or to at least not disappoint their fans' expectations.

And as poetic and romantic as the notion of a hockey team fighting for the home crowd is, it is only the last of those motivations — the bond with teammates — that truly wins enough games to define champions. The shared link of responsibility between teammates that is unique to a hockey team is one of the sport's most important elements. Individual talent is fine — and needed — to win games. But only a team wins a championship.

Contract maneuvering, personal statistics and the adoration of the neighborhood is faint in the mind of a champion as he sits in a locker room before a third period, deep in the playoffs, down by a goal. He looks down the row of sweaty, heaving bodies, into the eyes of his teammates. Do we want it? Will we do it? Will we try? Champions have the answers to these questions.

Barry Melrose, once of the Racers' rival Cincinnati Stingers, and later of NHL coaching and TV commentating fame, once defined his idea of "courage" in hockey terms during a 2003 ESPN broadcast: "Courage is when the puck is in the corner, you're smaller than the other guy who is going in after it, and you know it probably won't work out very well for you. But you know you need to do it for your teammates. That is courage."

As I grew up in Ohio and Indiana, I was taught the best of the stereotypical Midwest American values: that hard work is its own reward (and sometimes even pays off), that working together is the best way, that nothing comes easy and that caring for others when the going gets tough is the true mark of a man. And there's one more quality, perhaps one I learned from hockey: that we should try to find the courage within us, if we can.

So it's no wonder that these Indianapolis Racers — scratching, clawing and fighting, together — would capture my heart. It's no wonder that I would see mortal men, a young goaltender and a radio announcer, as my teenage heroes.

PUTTIN' ON THE GAME SEVEN FOIL

Racers' coach Jacques Demers' team-building attitude adjustment worked wonders — the under-talented Racers became tough, determined and competitive. Their march to the 1976 playoffs is as remarkable as it is improbable:

On February 22, 1976, they are in the WHA Eastern Division cellar, seven points out of the playoffs with only 20 games remaining, 12 of them on the road. Future Hall of Famer and former Toronto Maple Leafs great Dave Keon joins the club on March 14, and scores an assist in the 6-4 win over Phoenix. Indianapolis suddenly seems unstoppable: The 3-1 victory at New England on March 28 brings the Racers' unbeaten streak to 10 games, and vaults Indianapolis into first place for the first time in their history. There are four more regular season games to go, and the difference between last place and first place is razor thin.

Goaltender Jim Park extracts some personal vindication in his April 2 win at Maple Leaf Gardens. The Ontario native had previously been refused a tryout with the Toronto Toros, making the 3-1 win even sweeter. The next night, MSA registers its first 16,040 Racers sellout, though the Whalers spoil the party with a 5-2 win.

The Racers conclude the regular 1975-76 season on the road with a 4-2 win over New England, and they sit again in first place — with a precarious one-point lead over Cleveland, which still has one game remaining.

Only in the WHA could this last part of the story be true: The Cleveland Crusaders' last opponent, at home no less, was the San Diego Mariners. The Mariners had not been paid by owner Joseph Schwartz since March 19, and the team was currently being operated by the league itself. Amazingly, the Mariners beat Cleveland at the 7:49 mark of the 10-minute overtime.

Though finishing the regular schedule slightly under .500 (at 35W–39L–6T), the Racers won a decisive 12, lost four and tied four in their final heart-stopping 20 games of the season. So they entered the 1976 playoffs with a sense of well-fought accomplishment: The Indianapolis Racers were WHA Eastern Division Champions.

There was good news on the financial front, too. Reporter Wayne Fuson of the Indianapolis News wrote in April 1976, "Indianapolis' winning had paid off at the box office, naturally. Attendance for 40 home games this season averaged 8,878, an increase of some 13 percent. Since the Racers' surge began, however, the crowds at Market Square Arena have been well over 10,000."

Now on to virgin territory for Indianapolis: the playoffs. Their first round draw, the seasoned and former WHA champion New England Whalers, seemed to take the newly energized Racers lightly, and must have been surprised when they were extended to a deciding Game Seven. Indianapolis hosted the biggest game in its short history, and that's when the SuperFans were granted a couple of very funny visitors.

A couple New England players were scratched from that night's pivotal game. So with nothing to do but sit in the stands, they came up to the rafters to introduce themselves to, as they described us, "the nuttiest kids in the building." They were a flamboyant sight, with scraggly hair and loud plaid leisure suits. They were also dead-ringers for two-thirds of the foil-wearing, brawling "Hanson Brothers" from the classic 1977 comedy film "Slapshot." ("Hanson Brother" Steve Carlson told me in 2007 it couldn't have been them — they were filming the movie then, and only played with the Whalers in the following season.)

Whoever they were, they cracked jokes and were two of the nicest opposing players we had met. I asked countless questions about the Whalers, the minors and their life in hockey. They were happy to talk, and said they loved crazy fans like us because we made the games so much more interesting for them. It might seem odd that we had such a grand time with members of the "enemy" — during a deciding playoff game no less — but we relished the opportunity to talk with pro players.

The Whalers ruled that Game Seven with an iron fist, and the Racers' season started to tick away. Then, with about five minutes to play, something wonderful happened. The hometown Indy crowd, which had seemingly willed the Racers into the playoffs and into a Game Seven, showed the ultimate appreciation: one by one they rose to their feet, and thanked the team with a continuous roar. This was not just an expected "thank you" cheer from a home crowd at the end of a long season. This was a blast of emotion that I can still hear ringing today, decades later.

"Maybe that's what made the end of the Indianapolis Racers' second season so special to those of us who got to see it. Because for those brief moments there was Camelot," wrote Dave Overpeck afterward in the Indianapolis Star. "It may never come here again. But as it all came to an end Thursday, there was that magic, a feeling of affection that had both players and fans trying to comfort one another, and emotion that was very, very personal and unashamedly public.

"Only a little more than half of the 16,040 who started the night remained as the curtain came down. But in a way that made it better. These were the people who had been there all year and last season, too. They were the true believers, the all weather fans."

The buzz grew louder and louder — the Whaler players looked around in wonderment — they were ahead 6-0 and would win the series, wouldn't they? The roar lasted through the game's final whistle. I looked at my fellow SuperFans, Dave and Billy, with awe. The Racers were worth cheering about after all.

"The 8,500 or so who remained at Market Square Arena had been standing and cheering the Racers as they went through the painful but traditional ritual of shaking hands with the Whalers and then disappeared through the portal," Overpeck continued. "Now it was Demers' turn. And as he made the slow, lonely walk, the roar grew again, seeming to build higher and louder than ever, becoming as total a paean of affection as many can give unto one."

There had been talk of Demers jumping to a more stable coaching situation, but he said the next day to the Indianapolis News' Dick Denny, "You know when I really decided to stay as coach of the Racers? When I walked across the ice (at Market Square Arena) after we had lost by a 6-0 score Thursday night and heard all those people cheering me and the team. That walk seemed two miles long, but I've never been so emotionally touched in my whole life. No words can describe how I felt inside. I'm still emotional today."

Demers then told the Indianapolis Star, "I think the Racers are the survival of the WHA. I think everyone in the league right now realizes it's the greatest city in the WHA. Any player in the league would love to play here."

The Indianapolis Racers rose from a dismal inaugural season to a division championship and seven game playoff series — all in one year. Rookie goaltender Michel Dion also won the 1976 Ben Hatskin Award for Best Goaltender — with a 2.74 GAA — the second best goals-against average for the WHA's entire seven year history.

"There's no doubt Dion is superstar material," Demers told George Vass of the Hockey Digest after the 1975-76 season. "He proved conclusively last season he was the best goaltender in the league. With a power team, like the Jets, he would have won 50 games. With us he was under pressure every game yet he played remarkably well. There were no laughers because we don't score that many goals but we won in front of him because he came up with all the big saves."

But the best was yet to come. The Racers' stock was still rising.

"But always remember this hockey team," Dave Overpeck concluded in his May 1976 season wrap-up for the Indianapolis Star. "It's the one that made hockey here."

POWERPLAY: THE WHA vs. THE NHL

Indianapolis Racers fans would never get to share in the eventual fruits of the WHA's labors — the NHL's full-blown, wide open European style of pro hockey that the World Hockey Association made possible. We only got to see its prototype — when the WHA Winnipeg Jets came to town.

The Jets' trio of Anders Hedberg, Ulf Nilsson and Bobby Hull remains one of the most explosive lines I've ever seen in hockey — they were pure hockey joy, even when skating circles around my hometown team.

I met Bobby Hull in 2000, while serving as the radio play-by-play man and media director for a college hockey team. He seemed leery when I began to discuss the WHA — after more than 25 years of criticism and disdain from the NHL and its fans about his role in the WHA's inception, his caution was understandable. But his face softened when I thanked him for making the WHA possible, and then spoke with reverence about his Winnipeg teams and the integration of European players.

"We had some fine hockey teams in Winnipeg," Hull told me with a smile. "Great teams and great teammates." Then he leaned back, as if leaning back in time, and glanced sideways at me with his crooked hockey grin. "Those were good times, weren't they?"

Racers Captain Hugh Harris said in 2006, "The WHA really opened the door, not only for a lot of young kids, but if you go back and check the records, they also brought in the Swedes, they brought in the Finns.

"When the NHL took in the WHA teams that were going to stay around, they were really trying to get the European players that were well-rounded and could play anywhere. Before the WHA, they wouldn't give 'em the time of day. You know, your Hedbergs, your Nilssons — excellent players, especially in Winnipeg."

So how good was the WHA in comparison to the NHL? It's interesting to note the WHA won the majority of the more than 70 pre-season exhibition games against the NHL. The Winnipeg Jets, at the height of their WHA power, even challenged the mighty Montreal Canadiens to a four-game series, but were refused. The Canadiens had everything to lose in such a series — and the WHA won respect simply by making the challenge public.

An October 21, 1977 Racers game program story gloated, "The WHA, on the eve of its sixth season, after a summer during which a proposed merger of WHA teams into the NHL was rejected by the older league, accomplished at least as much as it hoped in its pre-season confrontations with the NHL."

WHA president Howard Baldwin said in the program's story, "If there is anyone in NHL cities who believed expansion involving our teams would weaken their league, they had better take another look at the record." In the 1977-78 pre-season exhibitions alone, the WHA won 13, lost 6 and tied two against the NHL. Seven of the wins were against NHL playoff teams from the previous season, five of the six WHA teams earned at least one win, and seven of the nine NHL teams lost at least once to the WHA.

"Lest anyone question the attitude that some NHL teams brought to these games, the finale, a 4-3 overtime triumph by the Québec Nordiques over the Washington Capitals, was scheduled only when Caps General Manager Max McNab issued a public 'challenge' to the WHA AVCO World Trophy Champions," the story continued.

"What we did prove, game in and game out, is that our teams can play with their teams. And we proved it indisputably," Baldwin said in the same program feature.

Former Minnesota Fighting Saints Coach Harry Neale summed it up best in a 2003 TV interview, noting, "Our league wasn't as good as we thought it was, but it was a lot better than the NHL thought it was."

The mainstream media was slow to accept the WHA as the NHL's equal in the league's first few seasons. While the league may not have withstood favorable comparison to the NHL during its first years from 1972-1975, there was no way to avoid the comparable quality of the leagues by 1976.

In late 1975 Christie Blatchford wrote in the Toronto Globe and Mail, "Face it, folks. There isn't much difference between the World Hockey Association and the National Hockey League, not anymore. When the two leagues each send one of their best clubs into town, it takes a picky man to still spot the big and blatant contrasts of a few years ago. They simply do not exist, not after three long seasons the WHA spent learning the ropes.

"It is likely, in the end, that the WHA will have given us as much quality hockey as the NHL. In fact, the real remaining difference between the two leagues may very well be in the way they are regarded in the press box. Sports reporters are still, in their hearts, refusing to acknowledge the WHA. It's time, really, to give up that kind of thing."

In my experience from the 1970s through today, it is interesting that the hockey fans or media people I've encountered who attempted to label the WHA as inferior all shared one thing in common: they did not follow both leagues and see actual games firsthand throughout the WHA's history. Quite simply, they weren't there and do not have firsthand knowledge — in the context of the times — to inform their opinions. (Of course, I also discount the self-interested rants from NHL owners or others with a financial stake in the relative status of the two leagues.)

I immersed myself religiously in both leagues throughout the WHA and Racers' five-year history, and was an NHL fan, too. I remain convinced: by 1976 the two leagues were extremely close in quality, and the best WHA teams would have been competitive and dangerous in the NHL playoffs.

Wayne Gretzky agreed on the league's quality, saying in the WHA history tome "Same Game, Different Name," by Jack Lautier and Frank Polnasnek, "The WHA had some tremendous young talent, probably as much as the NHL. The top 10 or 12 players on every team could have played in the NHL ... but that's something we'll never know."

Many WHA players who went on to stellar NHL careers have recognized the worth and importance of the rebel league. "The WHA is my roots, and I'm real proud of that," former Racers goaltender Ed Mio told Kevin Allen for the October 1998 Beckett Hockey Card Monthly magazine. "There was a lot of talk about how the WHA had goon squads and there was a lot of fighting, but the hockey was pretty good. I know I faced a lot of good shots."

Former Racers coach Jacques Demers agreed, telling Beckett, "That team in Winnipeg would have beaten a lot of teams in the NHL. They (the Jets' Swedish stars) got the stuffing kicked out of them, but they took the punishment and they were great players. That line was as good as you'll ever find."

Like most of the WHA veterans, Demers understood that opportunity was the upstart league's greatest legacy. "How can you be negative about the WHA? It got me to the NHL. It gave minor leaguers and Europeans a chance to play and sometimes doubled and tripled salaries of people. I really believe I never would have made it to the NHL without the WHA."

And the WHA gave very young players a jump start to their careers, preparing them for the eventual rigors of the NHL. "I felt playing pro hockey, playing against men, gave me the confidence, and I had an edge.

It was a stepping stone for a lot of young players, and it was exciting. A lot of players will tell you they owe a lot to the WHA," said former Racer Mark Messier in Ed Willes' book "The Rebel League."

The WHA also introduced some innovative rule changes to major league hockey, such as the overtime period in regular season games we now take for granted in the NHL.

The war between the leagues has been over for decades now — but the NHL will not finally give the WHA its well-earned respect and due in the record book. The reason for the long-lasting grudge is the very reason why the league was formed in the first place: money. The WHA's organizers claimed they formed their league to battle the injustice of the NHL's "reserve clause," which bound players to a team at artificially low salaries. The reality is that the WHA simply needed to create its own product to sell, and defeating the reserve clause in court was a business necessity. The NHL had locked out new owners and franchises for years, so the WHA had to find a way to create its own game. The answer was money — dangled in front of NHL players — and lots of it. The inflated salaries of the WHA, needed to lure players from the NHL, was simply the cost of creating business, not a kind-hearted gesture of sports justice.

And while the reserve clause and the WHA are both long gone, the avalanche of inflated salaries remains. The WHA's ghost still costs the NHL countless millions of dollars annually because of the players' rightful ability to sign free agent contracts — and that's why the rebel league will never get its due. "(Chicago Blackhawks) owner William Wirtz once estimated that increased spending for player salaries and minor league development, combined with huge legal bills and reduced attendance revenues cost the NHL roughly $1 billion over the lifetime of the WHA," wrote Murray Greig in his book "Big Bucks & Blue Pucks."

The final victory for the upstart league was the absorption of four WHA teams into the NHL in 1979. The ultimate irony for three of the teams involved in the merger — New England, Winnipeg and Québec — is that they were eventually forced to move their franchises allegedly because of the escalating costs of the free agent market — the problem created by the league that gave them life, the WHA.

The fourth former WHA team, Edmonton, has won a boatload of Stanley Cups — but still struggles annually to make ends meet as a small market franchise. Just like in the "good" old days.

The WHA did leave its mark in the NHL record books, in a roundabout way: For the six years after the merger, three of the top 10 NHL scorers were former WHA players with #1 Wayne Gretzky (1,337 points);

#8 Michel Goulet (634 points); #10 Kent Nilsson (622 points). The top two point producers in NHL history — Wayne Gretzky and Mark Messier — are former WHA Indianapolis Racers.

And the ultimate economic irony came within a newly designed WHA concept, proposed in 2003 and 2004 by various new developers of a re-born league. The original league was made possible by soaring salaries, but the new WHA proposed a tight salary cap designed to keep payrolls affordable. (To date this new major-league WHA has not appeared.) The NHL finally adopted a salary cap system, after their 2004-2005 lockout disaster, designed to address the endless salary escalator.

Maybe a new WHA — or another new challenger named something like the "Galactic Hockey Association" — will come by someday and steal NHL players again with higher salaries.

And then the financial nightmare — that WHA déjà vu — will be shared once again in all the league offices.

THE ARENA

The atmosphere at Market Square Arena grew legendary around Indianapolis, and in 1976-77 it was a hot local entertainment ticket. "Don't get the idea that we don't like to be the No.1 team in town," coach Jacques Demers told the Indianapolis News in April, 1976. "This hockey club has given something for the people here to talk about. Everywhere we go people are talking hockey." Ironically, though the basketball Pacers had triumphantly joined the National Basketball Association in the ABA-NBA merger of 1976, it was the hockey Racers who had captured the city's attention.

The official Racers Booster Club seemed largely responsible for the positive buzz the Racers enjoyed in Indianapolis. Rabidly loyal by any league's standards, it had a family atmosphere that reflected Indianapolis and its wholesome image perfectly. And the boosters, in their blazing Racers red windbreakers and ID buttons, seemed to be everywhere at MSA.

Booster Club officer Judy Stuart remembered how alive the stands in MSA became with the boosters' help. "My favorite memory of a player is Dale Smedsmo, when he was an opponent, and the sign in the stands, 'Smedsmo eats Alpo.' He'd get kicked out or scratched and it would take him five minutes (after changing clothes) to go up the stairs at MSA because he would stop and talk to everyone and particularly their kids." (The intimidating-looking Smedsmo would later play for the Racers.)

The "Positive Waves" battle cry from the previous season had expanded in the 1976–77 season with the ice skating Racers mascot named "Moriarity." Left untold, until now, is the fact that the Racers and their Booster Club got the "official" story of Moriarity completely wrong. The Moriarity mascot was said to be based on the character that actor Donald Sutherland played in the movie "Kelly's Heroes," who believed in "Positive Waves." But Sutherland's character was actually named Sgt. Oddball. It was another character, played by television veteran Gavin McLeod, who was the Moriarity character (spelled "Moriarty" in the movie and sometimes by the Racers) — and he was the most negative character in the movie. Sutherland's character was always complaining about Moriarty's *negative* waves."

So the Racers' "Positive Waves" battle cry of 1976 and 1977 — and their Moriarity mascot — is based on a monumental naming (and spelling) mistake. (Admittedly, "Sgt. Oddball" doesn't have the same good luck mascot ring to it, but high-school kids might have identified with that pot-smoking character better.)

Racers public relations director Walt Marlow was a fine journalist, but he was dead wrong when he wrote in a December 4, 1976 game program, "Nobody's laughing at Moriarity." The SuperFans laughed their heads off every time the carrot-topped monstrosity took the ice at Market Square Arena, before games and between periods, as he attempted to avoid being squashed by the circling Zamboni.

The team was more diplomatic, though. "Sure, the Moriarity thing was a factor," Hugh Harris told Marlow. "It's the power of positive thinking. We had the talent to win. But nobody can win if you're down on yourself."

The SuperFans loved that positive attitude, but just plain hated the Moriarity / Moriarty mascot. Its carrot-red yarn-hair and elf ears seemed especially un-cool to us teenagers, and we mercilessly made fun of it (much to the consternation of some adult "official" booster club members).

The costume head sat precariously high on top of a skater, who almost blindly staggered around the ice and stands; it seemed a feather could knock him over. The SuperFans would place bets with each other on how many times per game he would fall down, and we were not surprised when visiting Cincinnati fans once pummeled the defenseless ice-elf with punches on their way into a game in Indy. (The fellow inside the suit, identified as David Caldwell, was not hurt.)

So our apologies to all the kind-hearted fan club folks who thought up and constructed Moriarity. But it still makes us laugh.

AS FAR AS THEY COULD GO

There was no laughing in the Czechoslovakia national team dressing room after they dropped a hard-fought 3-2 game to the Racers on December 22, 1976. Considered one of the strongest national teams on the planet (behind the Russians), the win over the Czechs was psychologically gratifying, as the Racers matched the Europeans' style of play — and won. The WHA boldly scheduled European national teams for exhibition tours, and in the 1977-78 season these games even counted in the league standings. Games against the Russian teams were especially entertaining and generated great publicity for the league.

On the ice in regular play, the Racers had started the 1976-77 season slowly, as if suffering a hangover from the monumental turnaround of the previous year. They also would not sneak up on anyone in this new season — they held the unfamiliar role of favorites, as some picked them to win the Eastern Division over the powerful Québec Nordiques.

And the team's nagging money problems began to become more frequent and public. Paul Deneau had secured the club from the original owners in 1974, and now it was his turn to hit the road out of Indy. "The club came within a few hours of folding when Indianapolis Hockey Ltd. (headed by Deneau) didn't have the cash to make the November 1 payroll," Dave Overpeck wrote in the December 26, 1976 Indianapolis Star. "Only the sale of the club to Hockey Management, Inc. (headed by Harold Ducote & Tom Berry) kept it afloat."

Not all the franchise news was bad, though. "Gratifying is the increase in attendance at Market Square Arena. Through the first 17 dates (of the 1976-77 year), the Racers were leading the WHA in attendance with better than a 9,200 average — up about 1,600 over the last year at this time," Overpeck added.

The Racers also boasted a large contingent at the 1977 WHA All-Star game, with players Pat Stapleton, Michel Parizeau, Hugh Harris and Blair MacDonald, and Jacques Demers as coach of the Eastern squad.

Rivalry sells tickets, and the Cincinnati Stingers had quickly become the most heated rival for Indianapolis. The 110-mile proximity of the two cities also made the competition between the teams' fans natural. I joined one regular season road trip where close to 2,000 Racers fans caravanned to a Stingers game at Riverfront Coliseum. The atmosphere was electric, and the change of venues an exciting departure from MSA. But the

Racers didn't play especially well that night, and Kim Clackson skated in front of the Racers fan section to challenge us to cheer a little louder.

While we wished to believe our conceit of Indy's superiority as a franchise, it was obvious that both Indianapolis and Cincinnati would have made fine additions had they continued on to the NHL. The rivalry would have only gotten better both on and off the ice. But in 1977 our thoughts were only of the upcoming AVCO Cup playoffs, and the chance for WHA supremacy.

So the fans were delighted that the Racers qualified for the 1977 playoffs with Cincinnati as their first foe. The Stingers were a streaky and hot team, and had finished the season strong, three points ahead of Indy and in second place of the WHA Eastern Division. The Racers had proven to be wildly unpredictable that season.

Game One was as tight as the WHA would ever see — it became the longest playoff game in league history by the time Gene Peacosh won it for the Racers at 8:30 of the *third* overtime. The 108-minute loss seemed to break the Stingers' back, and the Racers were within a only few days of a four-game series sweep.

"Even before the game, we knew we were going to beat 'em," Hugh Harris remembered. Harris would also grease the psychological wheels and call attention to an opponent's tendency to dive and draw penalties. "Just a simple little thing like before the game started, before (referee) Bill Friday would drop the puck, I would go over and say, 'Bill, tell this guy over here, meaning (The Stingers') Dennis Sobchuk, 'They freeze the goddamn ice so you can stand up. If you want to go swimming, go to a swimming pool.' Well, their whole bench would go crazy! You know, 'What's this guy talking to the referee for, before the game,' you know? We just set the tempo."

The SuperFans also made the trip to Cincinnati for that April, 9, 1977 overtime classic. "At that first playoff game in Cincinnati we didn't have all our stuff, but we brought the banners. Some Stingers fan, who was not amused by us, ripped down one of our banners and he ran and stuffed it into a toilet. We didn't try to get it out!" Dave Pickering recounted in 2004 with much laughter.

Billy Pickering, the huskiest and most intimidating of the SuperFans, would sometimes step in to handle opposing fans who didn't share our teenage sense of humor. "That's exactly what happened in Cincinnati," Dave Pickering remembered. "In between one of the overtime periods in that playoff game, we were walking around the arena leading the Racers fans in cheers, and people were throwing cups at us, garbage, all kinds of stuff. And one guy jumped down in front of me like he was going to punch me — and Billy stepped in front of me and he backed down. That was the best rivalry — we'd get booed going in and going out, it was great!"

The Racers scooped up a 7-2 Game Two victory in Cincy on April 12, and headed home for Game Three. They seemed unstoppable. The other SuperFans and I could not contain ourselves — we had to go and give a pep talk to winger Brian McDonald. He had long been one of our Racers favorites, partly because he lived just a few blocks down the street from me in Northern Indianapolis — and also because he had announced that he would retire at the end of the current season. If we were going to show our appreciation for his years of hockey toil, there was no tomorrow.

We arrived at his door and started clapping and chanting. He finally came out, in T-shirt and boxer shorts, literally rubbing his eyes. He was very kind, patiently gave autographs, and thanked us for the good wishes. Then he promised that he'd try his best that night.

We had done our job — we had inspired Brian McDonald — or so we thought. It was only later, at the game, that we realized something important. After a long season and in the middle of an important playoff series, we had awoken McDonald from a needed game-day nap. Thirty-two years old at the time, at the end of a 14-year career, he must have desperately needed the rest. Fan guilt enveloped us — did we ruin McDonald's last playoff run?

That night Brian McDonald iced the Game Three win with a shorthanded, coast-to-coast goal that I will never forget. Picking up the puck behind his own goal on the penalty kill, he slowly weaved by one Stinger, then another, then another to center ice. A deke and he was at the blue line — one defenseman to go — then he dipped in front of the Stingers' goaltender. The biscuit sat in the back of the net.

Market Square Arena erupted into a frenzy, and I jumped so high that I tumbled down several rows of stairs from the SuperFans' usual perch at the top of the arena. Dave and Billy retrieved me, scooped me up, and held me high over the crowd. It seemed like I could fly.

That 20 seconds or so remains one of my most cherished hockey memories. Brian McDonald, a career grinder, was the poster boy for blue-collar Indianapolis, and for a few seconds he was invincible. He was selected as the playoff series MVP — a fitting reward for Brian McDonald's final days in hockey. When we heard of the award, Billy Pickering reminded me with an "of course" wink — "Brian told us he'd try his best."

In a TV interview after the series-clinching victory on April 16, 1977, a gracious McDonald declared to the camera lens that Indianapolis fans were the best. "We heard them chanting for us before we even went out for warm ups," he said. "The Cincinnati players were awed by them." The wild post-game scene in the stands that night seemed more like a championship party than simply the conclusion of the first playoff round, but Indy fans had suffered through the team's first few years — we cherished the time to revel in the results of our own "Positive Waves."

Stellar goaltender Michel Dion was also ecstatic, exclaiming to a TV reporter, "This whole week is probably the most perfect week the Racers ever had." He was right — the playoff series sweep against Cincinnati was the apex of the franchise. The Racers fell in the next round 4–1 to the eventual league winner Québec Nordiques, and never again tasted the sweet taste of championship possibility.

Defenseman Darryl Maggs was deservedly voted to the 1977 WHA year-end All-Star Team, and like Michel Dion's goaltending award from the previous season, this individual award was also a recognition of the intense defensive team effort that was the hallmark of the Racers' identity.

With playoff games included, the Racers finished the 1976-77 season at an exactly even 41–41–8 record and an average attendance just a hair under 10,000 fans — the best marks they'd ever achieve.

CONFLICT AS THE ESSENCE OF DRAMA

But the SuperFans' optimism was soon jolted. The daily newspapers reported that financial woes had plagued the team for almost its entire existence, but we realized that the franchise was truly in desperate trouble when the three most important Racers — coach Jacques Demers, goalie Michel Dion and star defenseman Pat Stapleton — were suddenly with the hated Cincinnati Stingers for the 1977–78 season.

By June of 1977, the Racers were without an owner yet again, and oblivion seemed days away. Racers fans waited to hear if there would be a 1977-78 season in Indianapolis. As the Indiana National Bank took receipt of the team finances, and searched for possible new ownership before declaring the enterprise dead, players and coaches were released to find work elsewhere. Demers waited as long as possible before signing on with Cincinnati, declaring almost daily in the Indianapolis newspapers his loyalty to the Racers, his tortured emotions about leaving — and the fear of the Racers players.

"As Hugh Harris said, they must have some answers. They are scared, really scared. I would say four or five of them have called me and said they definitely would like to play for me in Cincinnati. I've talked to the management there," Demers told the Indianapolis News.

Reiterating his belief in the city's hockey future, however, he told the Indianapolis Star on June 18 — even after he signed with the Stingers — "There's no question in my mind that Indianapolis is a great major league hockey city. You cannot blame non–fan support for what has happened here. They've supported us well."

Canadian real estate magnate Nelson Skalbania entered the picture at that last moment in June 1977 and according to published reports, bought his 51 percent controlling interest in the troubled team for one dollar, assuming all team debts. The fans and management alike hoped that this new owner would finally give the team the funds it needed to rekindle the hard-fought momentum of the previous two seasons. The fans also hoped that a new, well-financed owner could enhance Indianapolis' chance of being included in the possible merger between the NHL and WHA. Merger talks had been on and off between the leagues for years, but without solid ownership we knew that Indy wouldn't be included in any possible deal.

But timing is everything: if Skalbania had arrived even a few weeks earlier, then the nucleus of the Racers' best lineup could have been saved before the players signed with other clubs. In many ways, especially in the talent department, it was as if the Racers franchise would be starting over as an expansion team.

At least there would be a "next year."

"The Racers, showing more lives than a lucky cat, appear to have successfully not only dodged the fatal bullet but caught it in their gums — I mean teeth," wrote Racers Booster Club officer Tom Griffin in the opening night October 18, 1977 game program. "The cavalry once again has ridden to the rescue. In the role of John Wayne we have Nelson Skalbania, the 39-year-old real estate developer from Saskatchewan. The 7th Cavalry is comprised of David Givens and Larry O'Connor of Indiana National Bank. It is through the efforts of these three men that we still have hockey in Indianapolis."

But Skalbania, who admitted that he neither watched hockey nor knew the business of hockey, immediately dissolved whatever progress the franchise had achieved. In describing the kind of new general manager he would hire, he told the Toronto Globe & Mail in August 1977, "He doesn't have to know the difference between a basketball and a puck."

The team unity of the past two seasons was erased by Skalbania's subsequent roster hacking, and the talent pool in Indy would never be rebuilt. Skalbania's management seemed to stagger the Racers organization almost immediately, so it was no surprise that back on the ice, in the new season, they immediately sunk to last place in the standings. An absentee owner in the largest sense, it was reported in a Toronto Globe & Mail piece that the jet-setting Skalbania only bothered to see 10 of the team's 41 home games in 1977–78.

Many of the fan favorites who did survive the exodus to Cincinnati, including goaltender Jim Park, soon found disfavor under new Racers coach Ron Ingram. "A new coach comes in, and the goalie is the first person to get the blame, so you start wheeling goalies in and out and things become a mess," Jim Park said in 2004. "It was like they were already planning to fold it up."

Ingram brought with him some favorite players from his last WHA stop in San Diego, and by all accounts took former Racers coach Gerry Moore's dour personality and doubled it. One former player even noted he was not sorry to hear that Ingram had passed away in 1988. Old grudges die hard, even if old coaches are already dead.

By mid-season, Ingram was fired, and former NHL star Bill Goldsworthy took over as player-coach. Ingram held on technically as the team's general manager, but had left the building for the last time by March. Harvey Rosen reported in a winter 1978 edition of the Winnipeg "Jet Stream" booster newsletter that in Indy, Ingram's "wife and daughter were forced to change their seats when fans began to abuse them verbally. Ron's car is spat upon, the air is let out of his tires, and obscenities are written on his dust-covered vehicle." All was not well within the Racers' faithful.

"You got to remember the team was in kind of a, I wouldn't say disarray, but they'd just come from a good season with Jacques Demers, and things just weren't happening," said goaltender Ed Mio in 2006. "We didn't have the type of players, we had a good nucleus but we just weren't playing well. So when Bill (Goldsworthy) inherited it, he had the old good NHL mentality, where you try and make it fun and 'We're there, let's just try and play games and build for the end of the year.' So the atmosphere was actually pretty good."

The personnel exodus to Cincinnati continued, however. Captain Hugh Harris, defensive star Darryl Maggs, Reg Thomas and Bryon Baltimore — fan favorites one and all — would all end up wearing the Stingers' gold and black that season via trades.

On the ice, no matter who was in the lineup, there wasn't much to cheer about, although Rusty Patenaude was a worthy selection for the 1978 WHA All-Star game.

The SuperFans, positive as always, were unfazed by the relative lack of season highlights. "Even if it was a stinker of a game, we'd find something positive to talk about," Dave Pickering said. "I remember one game where Houston crushed the Racers 10–0, and we kept cheering — we wouldn't give up on our guys! And I remember knowing almost everyone on the Whalers and Aeros and Stingers, because I saw them so often. They didn't give us any problems — they knew we were real fans."

The Racers even featured the SuperFans in a late 1977 game program article, and we were stunned — suddenly we were right next to our beloved boys in red, white & blue. But I told my SuperFan brothers, "I have a no-trade clause in my contract. I will refuse to report to Cincinnati if traded." Much laughter ensued.

Other fans hadn't given up on their team, either. Dedicated Racers supporter Judy Shaver remembers the boosters' marathon weekend trip with the team to Houston and Winnipeg in January 1978. In Houston, "The fan club sat together behind one of the nets. It so happened that Nelson Skalbania was sitting by me. During the game, he asked me how I liked the scoreboard hanging down in the middle of the rink and the instant replay. He told us he would get one for Market Square Arena." The Racers honored the fans' long-distance devotion with a 2-1 win on January 7, 1978.

After winter storms in Canada, jet problems and Customs snafus (and a 4-2 loss at Winnipeg on January 8), Shaver didn't get back to Indianapolis until Monday morning. So she did what any normal hockey fan and first-grade school teacher would do — she drove straight to work in her Racers jersey. Shaver playfully calls the adventurous international trek — filled with memories of the amiable Racers, friends and fans — her "lost weekend."

Another fun diversion from the on-ice woes of 1977-78 was the SuperFans' public feud with Channel 13 TV sportscaster Pete Liebengood. The sports anchor didn't seem to care much for the Racers, and during one broadcast he took jabs at their fans — specifically the rowdy kids at the top of Market Square Arena — the SuperFans.

As a budding journalist and an editor of my North Central High School newspaper, I knew I could have some fun if we upped the battle of words. I called the TV station's general manager and demanded equal air time to defend the Racers and their fans. They went for it, which was their first mistake.

With another school reporter and photographer in tow, we went to Channel 13 and I taped my written statement, while Liebengood needled us. "We were constantly harassed by one insulting barb after another," Sports Editor Alex Waddell wrote in the resulting December 16, 1977 "Northern Lights" newspaper piece. We sent the station general manager a copy of the story — hell hath no fury like a bunch of snotty teenage journalists.

But the fun was just beginning. The bizarre TV station clash with Liebengood inspired us to poll 300 North Central High students about their favorite — and least favorite — Indianapolis sportscaster. Liebengood grossed one-half of the negative votes and "won" the most-disliked category by a landslide! Since he probably wasn't going to put us on his show with the results, we instead turned to Channel 6 sports anchor Craig Roberts, the winner of the "favorite sportscaster" poll category.

Roberts was a Racers supporter, and surviving on-air footage of Roberts interviewing players shows he was a knowledgeable sportscaster, too. He welcomed us warmly to the Channel 6 studios for an on-camera presentation of the winner's plaque, amazed that he finished ahead of the venerated "Hockey Bob" Lamey in the voting.

Liebengood never bothered us or the Racers again.

Surly local media were the least of the Racers' problems, though. Owner Nelson Skalbania continued to mismanage the Racers, and the organization was unraveling. It was becoming clear, both inside and outside the team: Nelson Skalbania wasn't the Indianapolis Racers' savior, as was hoped only a few months before.

He was its executioner.

THE NUMBERS ARE ABOUT TO CHANGE

The Indianapolis sun blazed in the summer of 1978, and I squinted in my backyard as I tried to read a biography of goaltending pioneer Jacques Plante (who also ended up in the WHA). I took a break and turned to the Indianapolis newspaper, hoping to read of progress in the seemingly endless WHA-NHL merger talks. Instead, a large display advertisement seemed to scream something like: *The numbers in hockey are about to change*. The photo showed the back of a Racers jersey, with a "99" stitched onto it. The name on the jersey was "Gretzky." The Plante biography would have to wait.

Even with the resulting media hype over this teenage rookie — who was my same age, weight and height — the SuperFans' enthusiasm for the upcoming 1978–79 Racers was muted. Like many other hardcore fans, we suspected that the team roster had been gutted yet again. There was little, if any, practical thought that the franchise would complete the upcoming season.

But hope springs eternal in Indianapolis — and hope was needed as the season's first player payroll date grew near — so SuperFan Dave Pickering thought that just maybe Gretzky could save the day. "I think I was naïve, but I did. All that summer (1978) everything was 'Gretzky, Gretzky!' and merger talk was all the rage — we thought since the (basketball) Pacers were able to get into the NBA (in 1976) that there was still a chance that the Racers could get into the NHL. Our family went to the Hockey Hall of Fame in Toronto that summer and looked with awe at the Stanley Cup — 'What if one day the Racers could play for it?'— we actually said that out loud.

"And I asked a guy working there, 'So what do you think about Gretzky signing with Indianapolis?' And his response was, 'He can't skate!'" Pickering laughs at the assessment, which today, of course, couldn't be more ludicrous.

A curious sideshow then interrupted our digestion of the teenage Gretzky signing: On July 11, it was announced in the media that WHA Birmingham Bulls owner John Bassett had "reached an agreement in principle" to merge his club with the Indianapolis Racers. Bassett said he was running out of money, knew he would be left out of the imminent WHA–NHL merger, and that combining finances and rosters with Skalbania made the most sense. Yes, it did make sense — but two days later Bassett reversed course and said he had changed his mind: Birmingham would play the 1978-1979 season.

For most of the WHA's existence, merger talks with the NHL had been on again and off again, almost certain and never to happen, just around the bend and far in the distance — impossible to predict. It was the worst kept secret in hockey, though, that Indianapolis had never been seriously considered for the merger, and the franchise did not make formal applications for entry into the NHL as most of the other WHA clubs had. Since Indianapolis would not be included in the merger between the two major hockey leagues, the SuperFans asked ourselves: what was the purpose of the Racers even playing this last season?

Theory number one: "Skalbania simply wanted to keep his moribund franchise alive long enough to recoup his costs through the buy-out money he would receive in the event of a WHA–NHL merger…," Scott Adam Surgent writes in his book "The Complete Historical and Statistical Reference to the WHA."

The June 1978 signing of Gretzky added to the confusion, though. Why would Skalbania sell his interest in the Edmonton Oilers — a WHA team likely to be included in the merger — and then buy Indianapolis, a financially disastrous team that would not be included? Why sign 17-year-old star prospect Gretzky to a whopping contract (reported at between $1.125 million and $1.75 million) for a supposedly cash-strapped team?

Theory number two: The NHL prohibited the signing of players under 20 years of age, so Skalbania could beat the gold rush by signing the future "Great One" years before any NHL team could. It was also believed that the NHL would eliminate WHA teams from consideration if they signed underage players in anticipation of the merger. So a patsy team was needed to park Gretzky until the merger was worked out — then Gretzky could be moved to one of the WHA merger teams and enter the NHL the following year. And perhaps Skalbania still owned part of the Oilers.

That patsy team seemed to be the Indianapolis Racers. Gretzky became the ultimate pawn to help force the NHL to absorb WHA teams, but this intrigue also ensured that Indianapolis would be sacrificed.

Even Gretzky's father knew that his son's stay in Indianapolis was merely a stopover. "New England was out of the running for Wayne, but the WHA still wanted to sign him in order to keep the pressure on for a merger with the NHL," wrote Walter Gretzky in his 1984 book "Gretzky." "The logical team was Indianapolis, because with attendance as bad as it was the Racers didn't figure to be one of the teams taken in the NHL anyway."

For the record, the Racers averaged over their life almost exactly the same per–game attendance as the entire league, nearly 8,000, with a playoff average of more than 12,000 fans. New England, accepted into the NHL, averaged only 500 more fans a game than Indianapolis.

The Whalers might have been out of the Gretzky picture, but the Houston Aeros — who made good on a threat to fold when a merger with the NHL didn't take place that summer — could have re-surfaced if Skalbania took the boy-wonder to Texas. "At the time, believe it or not, it was Houston or Indianapolis," Wayne Gretzky revealed to Terry Jones of the Edmonton Sun in April 1999. "When I wrote the contract out on the plane, it had 'Houston or Indianapolis' on the contract. At the time, Nelson was negotiating to buy Houston. Gus (Badali, Gretzky's agent) was pushing big time for it to be Houston."

Wherever the teenage Gretzky would eventually land, his million-dollar signing was scandalous in the 1978 hockey world, and brought gasps throughout the Canadian junior leagues.

"All my life, I've worked toward becoming a professional hockey player. If I didn't sign and next year went back (to juniors) and broke my leg, then I couldn't say I played pro hockey," Gretzky explained to the Toronto Globe & Mail on June 13, 1978.

Gretzky's agent, Gus Badali, added to the justification (as retold in the 2003 book "Messier"), "There's a war between two leagues, and I'm an agent with a client. How can I tell Wayne that he should not take nearly a million dollars from Indianapolis and go back to the Soo (Sault Ste. Marie Greyhounds) for $75 a week?"

Even after he signed with Skalbania, Indianapolis wasn't on Gretzky's hockey radar. "Then Indianapolis came up and I had no idea where Indianapolis was," Gretzky said in "The Rebel League," a book by Ed Willes. "It was awkward in Indianapolis. I was a 17-year-old kid trying to find my way, and there were players on the team a lot better than me. But they were marketing the team around me."

The marketing was not effective. Skalbania quipped, in the same book, "I think our season ticket sales jumped 2,000 to 2,300 when we signed Wayne. A 17-year-old-kid, no matter how good he was, wasn't going to sell tickets in that market." In defense once again of the Indianapolis hockey fan, there was not one city in the world that would have lined up for major-league season tickets based on the exploits of an unproven teenage amateur rookie.

Skalbania himself never saw Gretzky skate for the junior Sault Ste. Marie Greyhounds, and had no idea of his existence until others in the WHA told him the signing could become a money-maker. And, according to newspaper accounts, there was still wide-spread disagreement, both throughout the WHA and NHL front offices, whether Gretzky was an actual pro prospect at all, let alone a sure-thing superstar. Some GMs believed that Gretzky would never play a game in the NHL.

In an October 27, 1978 Hockey News cover story, Gretzky played nice and contended he was accepted by his Racers teammates and did not feel overly pressured by the "Great Gretzky" ad campaign that tied the franchise's survival solely to him and his fan appeal. But he acknowledged to the Toronto Globe & Mail — after he left the Racers — "I knew that if Indy started out drawing not too well, then they'd have to make a move."

Teenage Racers fan Bruce Boggess remembered in 2004 that Gretzky was hardly overwhelmed by his fan club responsibilities. "One time after school I went over to Glendale Mall, and walked by one of the inner entrances to Ayres department store and saw Gretzky sitting there. Ayres had sponsored a fan club for him, and he was there to sign autographs. The strange thing was that other than a girl who was there from the store to keep him company, there wasn't anyone within a hundred feet of him. As I walked past the entrance he was looking around and laughing and looked right at me shaking his head, practically shrugging his shoulders as if to say, 'Anyone?'"

The headline for the October 27, 1978 Hockey News cover story, complete with a color photo of Gretzky in his Racers blues, was a more accurate barometer of the larger business pressure surrounding him: "Gretzky Big Hope For WHA's Future." Quite simply, if someone in the WHA had not signed Gretzky, then a merger with the NHL might never have happened.

The heat on the NHL to accept the WHA and finally merge the two leagues was finally at a boiling point, even in the news media. In that same edition of The Hockey News alone, headlines screamed, "WHA Teams Overshadow NHL by Winning Pre-Season Play," "New Faces Lift Racers, Stingers to Exhibition wins against NHL," and "Whalers Show NHL How It's Done."

But Indianapolis was destined to be left at the pro hockey altar. "I don't think we thought Indianapolis would be included (in a league merger) because there were a lot of rumors going when we started the year, even though we had Wayne, that we might be a team that was in trouble," said goaltender Ed Mio.

In hindsight, it's easy to see that Skalbania's habit since 1978 — buying and quickly folding or selling multiple sports teams — began with Edmonton and Indianapolis in the WHA. "Skalbania remains Canada's most prolific sports franchise owner," wrote Bob Mackin in the March 10, 2003 edition of the Vancouver Courier. "He flipped teams and players like kids used to flip hockey cards at recess."

In 1978, though, this new team owner's modus operandi was just taking shape. The SuperFans guessed that Skalbania would end up selling Gretzky back to the team he either still owned or formerly owned or would own part of again — Edmonton — and then fold the Racers while the cries of team debt still rang inside Market Square Arena. It's vital to understand that Gretzky wasn't signed to the Indianapolis Racers — he was owned by Skalbania through a personal services contract. We believed that the personal services contract helped guarantee that the Gretzky transaction would remain separate from the rest of the team.

"In truth Gretzky, not the Racers, was the franchise Skalbania owned," Douglas Hunter wrote in "The Glory Barons" book, in an excerpt included on the Edmonton Oilers' Web site. "All Skalbania had to do now was to keep the Racers afloat long enough to become part of the renewed merger negotiations with the NHL." WHA teams not included in the merger would be paid millions of dollars in a settlement, but the Racers' operational costs to Skalbania continued to pile up as negotiations between the leagues wore on. The best scenario for Skalbania would have been a merger before the 1978-79 season, with the selling of Gretzky to the NHL before he ever donned a Racers uniform. But that didn't happen, so he had to pony up more cash to put the team back on the ice in hopes that the eventual settlement money would be greater than his expenses.

Skalbania was also the object of bewilderment from his own players. "What was really degrading was when Nelson Skalbania had his daughter behind the bench on the some of the road games. I really don't know what the idea there was," said defenseman Ken Block. "When you experience something like that, you wonder, 'What is the motive for doing it?'"

Whatever Skalbania's motivations were with the Racers, most press did not believe that Gretzky's presence would have any effect on the team's on-ice fortunes. "Indianapolis has center Wayne Gretzky, but not much more," Kathy Blumenstock wrote in the 1978-79 Sports Illustrated WHA season preview on October 23, 1978. "The Racers signed 'Great Grits' to a seven-year, $1.7 million pact after the 17-year-old flash scored 70 goals last season for the amateur Sault Ste. Marie Greyhounds. Whatever he does for the Racers, Gretzky cannot possibly do enough to cover up the WHA's worst defense."

BUT CAN HE SKATE?

When training camp opened in September 1978 head coach Pat "Whitey" Stapleton was impressed. "It was a treat to coach Wayne Gretzky when he first came up with the Racers," Stapleton said in Murray Greig's book, "Big Bucks And Blue Pucks." "We could all see right away that he was something special. He had that extra sense, and he challenged defensemen like a seasoned veteran. I was also impressed with his maturity. He was only 17 and he'd just signed a million-dollar contract, but it didn't go to his head. He'd had a certain amount of notoriety for long time already, but being the center of attention in Indianapolis didn't faze him one bit. He was always very humble, very polite. I remember thinking that Wayne's parents did a great job in raising him."

Despite the kind words, Gretzky's father Walter didn't approve of Whitey's coaching style. "He was a good coach and a considerate man — too considerate for Wayne in his situation," Walter Gretzky wrote in his 1984 book "Gretzky." "He was so conscious of Wayne's welfare that he was determined not to put him in a pressure situation where people would expect wonders of him right away. I really believe that if Whitey hadn't been concerned — for all the best reasons — and had just turned Wayne loose from the start, he'd have blossomed right away."

Former Racers forward Al Karlander was invited to assist Stapleton behind the bench, and saw that despite all best efforts, Stapleton did not have the front-office managerial support any pro coach needs to succeed. "Whitey lost his energy in the coaching pretty early. He was GM/Coach, he was trying to do everything, and you know like I say, the business management team there was totally incompetent and didn't really work with Whitey very well. He was trying to run the hockey part of the operation within an environment of people who were totally incompetent in all aspects."

Karlander also saw firsthand that Skalbania's business style was certainly not open and inviting. "I sat in on one meeting with Nelson Skalbania at the Columbia Club and I asked him a couple of hard questions, and the representative sitting next to me leaned over and said that old quote, 'You were looking for employment when you took this job, weren't you Al?' You didn't ask those kinds of questions."

Gretzky and the Racers started the season painfully, and the Racers had no time for a slow start. At least he made it through his first pro training camp with the respect of some veterans. "I think everybody on the team is quite pleased with the way he's working," Racers backstopper Gary Inness told the Hockey News in October 1978. "He's feeling his way along, but he's got the moves. Anytime he touches the puck, he's a threat."

Assistant Coach Karlander's first impressions were more cautious. "First of all, it was a little bit of surprise at first at how young he was and how small he was. And you know, unless you were a knowledgeable hockey player or a knowledgeable hockey person, and watched him, you really would have questioned — like this is a joke, right?

"Unless you could see the mind, how his mind worked, because he certainly didn't dominate in any other fashion," Karlander continued. "It was totally the mental part of the game. I mean, he was 17 years old, so when he was out there, you think, 'He's small, he's slow, he doesn't shoot that hard,' these type of things. But when he was out there, it did seem like he was in control, particularly when he had the puck. At that point, with the puck was where he really stood out. Without it, he wasn't beating people and he was obviously trying to find his time and space in the game."

The future "Great One" did score a goal and assist in his first Market Square Arena exhibition game against the rival Cincinnati Stingers, a 5–5 tie on October 4, 1978. Two nights later in MSA the Racers defeated the NHL St. Louis Blues 4-1, and Gretzky added an assist.

Blues coach Barclay Plager told the Hockey News in the October 27, 1978 edition, "He must be a talented player. He didn't look out of place. I think 17 is a little young to start. The guys up here are so much bigger and stronger. But who knows when to start?"

The win against the NHL Blues seemed to be an early season rallying cry for the re-grouping Racers. "They're not the Montreal Canadiens, but they're still an NHL club," Gary Inness, himself a former NHL Philadelphia Flyer, told the Hockey News after the win. "We played NHL style hockey and we beat them at it. It should do a lot for our confidence." New Racer Don Larway, who scored a goal in the win, added, "Our biggest problem is psychological. Physically and fundamentally, we're 100 percent."

But Skalbania was not behind his financially floundering team 100 percent — he was about to quit bailing water. He even neglected to pay St. Louis the promised $25,000 for coming to Indianapolis to play, according to the Blues' Emile Francis in the book "Same Name, Different Game." Francis added that the Blues were only paid years later when Skalbania and a proposed ownership group solicited the NHL for the Calgary franchise — and Francis sat in the room for the presentation.

While some players and coaches were generous in welcoming the teenager, the Gretzky signing didn't create smooth waters up and down the lineup. Longtime Racers player Ken Block was gracious when discussing all his former teammates, including Wayne Gretzky, but did observe in 2006, "I think at the time, the thing that bothered me more was that he didn't sign a contract to play for the Indianapolis Racers, he signed a personal services contract with Nelson Skalbania. But when that's your team, and you're playing for the Racers, you have to be loyal to the team. And you're under contract, so you can't say, 'Geez, this is a red flag, I'm going to…' — because you don't have any options."

Still, it was a special night, October 14, 1978, when Gretzky debuted in a Racers jersey for his first regular season game, against Bobby Hull and the mighty Winnipeg Jets. I begged my SuperFan brothers for forgiveness — I had to sit near the ice to see his first game up close. He didn't have much impact that night — his nerves must have been enormous. But the Racers actually existed, and he was skating in our red, white and blue.

Coach Pat Stapleton, in a special four-page foldout that was inserted loose into the opening night program, attempted to soothe the worried nerves of Racers fans. "Where will the Racers finish this season? Frankly, I wish I could tell you," he wrote. We could not have known that night how wildly inaccurate his next comments would prove to be: "The Racers organization has a deep commitment to this city and state. I feel very strongly about the future of Indianapolis."

Gretzky didn't score his first pro goal against Winnipeg, but in a strange twist of hockey history fate Bobby Hull scored his last WHA goal that night in Indianapolis in the Jets' 6-3 victory. (Hull would sit out the bulk of remaining season, returning to play briefly after the two leagues merged the following year.)

The rookie Gretzky notched an assist (at Québec) two games later, then his first professional goals, at home in Indy, a game after that on October 20, 1978.

"They were both against Edmonton," Gretzky told Terry Jones of the Edmonton Sun in April 1999. "They were both on Dave Dryden. Twenty years later someone sent me a tape of my first two goals against Edmonton, and I'm looking at them with my kids and my young boys were laughing at me. They said I looked like I was a little kid." There's a reason for that; at age 17, though a millionaire and a professional hockey player, it is easy to forget that Wayne Gretzky was closer to being a little kid than a hardened veteran.

"He was just a skinny, frail-looking kid on the ice, but he toyed with players even then," former Racers coach Jacques Demers told Beckett Hockey Card Monthly magazine in 1998. "When Skalbania brought Gretzky to the WHA, he made a big deal about stealing him from the NHL. Everyone knew how important he was to the league."

Any sense of gloating in the Racers' front office over the signing coup was short-lived. Just a week after Gretzky's regular season debut, Skalbania told the Toronto Globe & Mail, on October 21, "I don't know why the hell I did that Gretzky deal."

Within a week, other newspapers reported the team could fold at any moment. "It's only in danger of folding if we couldn't get anybody locally to invest, and if Nelson (Skalbania) would walk away," club president Robert Johnston said in an Associated Press story on October 26. That scenario, of course, is exactly what would happen six weeks later.

Racers fans who figured out even a part of this shell game were not amused by their roles as an audition audience — the games in Indianapolis were now a stage for other owners and the NHL to gauge the market value of Gretzky (and the rest of the players) for the impending franchise fire sale.

I must note that the ill feelings and frustrations from the fans were not directed at Wayne Gretzky. We all realized he was just a young player — at my own age of 17 no less — and we guessed that he didn't have a part in these backroom franchise machinations. But it was doubly hurtful to the fans to have this budding superstar dangled in front of us as the franchise's savior, when it appeared there was no actual intention of continuing the team.

Wayne Gretzky played only eight regular season games with Indy in the fall of 1978, scoring three goals and three assists. (Interestingly, he led the team in scoring for the pre-season, with five goals and four assists in just six games.) I saw Gretzky off the ice once during his short stay, when he drove his new sports car to my high school campus to talk with some girls in between classes. He was technically enrolled at nearby Broad Ripple High School for classes two nights each week; perhaps the best-looking girls didn't attend night classes.

Any dates made that day would have to be broken: as predicted, Gretzky was soon sold (for a reported $850,000) to Edmonton on November 2, 1978 — along with goaltender Ed Mio and forward Peter Driscoll. Interestingly, that trio had been together in Indianapolis since before the start of the season.

Mio explained in 2006, "Peter (Driscoll) and I were called by Pat Stapleton a little earlier in the summer asking if we could come back to Indy because Wayne was coming in early in August and they were going to put him kind of close to where we were staying — Peter had just bought a house and we were living together, and Wayne was only going to be about a mile away, maybe not even a mile, half a mile, with a family.

"So we came in, we got to know Wayne a little bit before everybody else did, you know, going out and taking care of him. I think school started early in Indy, so again we had a whole month with Wayne before September, so that was just a way to get to know him.

"He was a great kid, we had no problem with him as far as individuals," Mio continued. "We still hadn't seen him skate, but the accolades were just too great to ignore coming out of Canada. So we were excited to watch him play, too. We got a little bit of insight to Wayne and his personality and his demeanor early, so we were quite impressed with the young guy and as it turned out we all got sold together. So it was something that — I don't know if they planned it that way or knew that we would be the three to leave early on — but they had us start a relationship with Wayne in August."

After leaving Indianapolis, Gretzky could reveal, in a sly way, some insight about his brief tenure in Indy by commenting on his relief to play in Edmonton. "I didn't feel like I had to sell hockey there (Edmonton)," he said in the 2004 "Rebel League" book. "And the other players didn't look at me like, 'Who's this kid making all that money?'" (Indy players did not nickname Gretzky "The Great One." They called him "Brinks," referring to the armored cash truck.)

It appears Gretzky holds few nostalgic ties to the team which gave him his pro hockey birth. In a Home & Garden network TV show tour of his California mansion it was revealed he has the logo crests of each of the pro teams he played for carved into his ceiling — all except the Indianapolis Racers.

The psychology might be simple: Gretzky went on to win Stanley Cups, scoring titles, MVP awards, and the rightful title of "The Great One." He is the most important hockey player of all time. In his entire hockey career, he has one great defeat, when he was involved in the failure of an entire franchise: The Indianapolis Racers. The first advertisement campaign of his pro career was based on Wayne Gretzky scoring goals and drawing fans. It didn't happen, he was sold like meat, and the remaining team soon erased. After all of that, I might tell the engraver to skip that Indy logo on my personal Hall of Fame ceiling, too.

We don't know more about what Wayne Gretzky thought of his time in Indianapolis or his knowledge of the peculiar backroom dealings concerning him and his entry into pro hockey. In 2005, Gretzky, by then the head coach and a part owner of the NHL Phoenix Coyotes, refused through his team media representatives my requests for as little as a 10-minute interview for this book. Repeated interview requests were made and denied regularly from late 2005 up until the completion of this book in 2007. After I interviewed Coyotes President Doug Moss in March 2007 for a major newspaper series on hockey in Arizona, Gretzky finally did agree to consider three questions, submitted in writing — and then he refused to answer them.

Timing could be part of the denial of access to "The Great One" — my first interview request took place in 2005 just as a hockey betting scandal involving a Coyotes assistant coach was about to break publicly. Gretzky went into a public relations bunker about most anything other than a current Coyotes game. Gretzky has since left the Coyotes amid more controversy — and refused again in 2012 repeated interview requests for this book's revised edition.

Decades earlier, back in November 1978, at least some of the remaining Racers didn't care one way or another that "The Great One" had departed. "I'm getting bored with this," Richie Leduc told the Associated Press on November 4, 1978. "Every time I get in the dressing room, it's 'What Nelson Skalbania is saying, or Stapleton is thinking.' I'd rather talk hockey and who we're playing tonight." Blaine Stoughton mentioned in the same piece that the Gretzky sale would simply mean more playing time for him.

At least for a few more weeks.

A FEW MOMENTS WITH MOOSE

Having the briefest glimpse of the teenager who would become hockey's greatest player is a strange enough footnote for the Racers — but how about an encore? Shortly after Gretzky disappeared from the Indy roster, another brash 17-year-old took his place: Mark Messier, later known affectionately as "Moose."

"In the wake of the sale of the Boy Wonder (Gretzky), the Racers extended a five-game trial Thursday to St. Albert Saints forward Mark Messier," wrote Jim Matheson in the November 3, 1978 Edmonton Journal.

Mark Messier's father, Doug, helped make the deal. "When Indianapolis lost Gretzky, I called my old defense partner Pat Stapleton and asked him to take a look at Mark," the elder Messier told the New York Daily News' John Dellapina in 2003. "He was going to get in trouble in our (junior) league — he was a little too physical." Interestingly, Doug Messier had played minor league hockey in Edmonton, Indianapolis and Cincinnati. He also spent time in Portland, Oregon in the Western Hockey League with Pat Stapleton from 1963-65.

The five-game tryout was part of two Racers road trips. Mark Messier's Racers debut was November 5, 1978 at Winnipeg. He went on to Cincinnati and Québec, then back to hometown Edmonton on November 17. Whitey Stapleton commented in the 2003 book "Messier" that the young rookie played "Well enough to play pro hockey," while he also prophetically caught the eye of Edmonton coach Glen Sather. (Fast-forward to Messier, Gretzky and Sather together holding the Stanley Cup with the NHL Edmonton Oilers, four times from 1984-1988. Moose would add two more Cups to his resume, in 1990 and 1994.)

Amazingly, after those four initial WHA games, Messier went back to his junior St. Alberts team to play, then finished his pro stint with Indy on November 28 at Edmonton. Messier declined to sign for more than a five-game tryout, so he had the option of keeping his amateur status and could return to the juniors — which is what he did, at least for a short while.

The brief audition did not lead to a season-long roster spot for Messier with Indianapolis, or even a home jersey. It didn't even earn him spending money — according to Doug Messier in the New York Daily News, his son's one paycheck from the Racers bounced.

But he had outgrown junior hockey for good, and soon he would sign with the Cincinnati Stingers for the remainder of that last WHA season. Then it would be on to Edmonton and the NHL.

The rest of the story for Mark Messier, as they say, is Hall of Fame hockey history.

DEATH RATTLES

As the Racers stumbled from venue to venue in November 1978, Stapleton and Skalbania were selling what they could of their roster, leaving a skeleton of a team. "It's been almost a month since we won," Stapleton told the Winnipeg press on November 20. "It seems like four years."

A week later, an unnamed Racers official told the Winnipeg press after a 5-1 loss to the Jets in Indianapolis, "We've got to get some players. It's senseless operating this way. We've got only seven players in our lineup who can play in this league. About five others are borderline. The rest are crap."

Veteran goaltender Gary Smith recounted a perfect example of Skalbania's bewildering management style, telling the Toronto Globe & Mail on November 17, 1978, "Nelson called us together to a meeting. This was right after he sold Wayne and the club wasn't going too well. He said, 'I thought you guys would play better hockey if you were worried about putting meat on your table.' He didn't understand how hard it is to live with all this uncertainty over where your next meal is coming from."

All Stapleton could do was throw up his arms. "What can I tell them?" he said in the same report. "I try to remind them that they have their future at stake, that they're playing with their careers on the line."

We closed our eyes and waited for the end. About this time I started to have a very peculiar dream, one that still visits me:

I am high above a hockey rink, at one end, watching the ice below through a wide horizontal window. Everything is white. A cloud of fog envelopes the ice, but I can see shadowy figures, some in white, some in blue, starting to stir, to circle around the edge of the rink. I watch it all serenely, reclining on a tilted bed, the perfect angle to watch it all, only having to move my eyes. The fog lifts as the players circle, and then they face off for a game. The puck echoes off the boards, off the goal posts, off clacking sticks. All the power plays produce goals, all the pucks are stopped by the goaltenders, and the players are never hurt, tired, or broke. It is hushed, graceful. I often wonder if it is my mind's idea of heaven.

Then my plastic AM radio alarm clock buzzed — I was late again for high school. The frozen Indiana snow crunched below my feet as I rushed to the school bus. I slid over a long patch of ice on the sidewalk, as if skating — and ended up flat on my back, hard. I stared at the white winter sky, trying to catch my breath. It was December 15, 1978, and my dream was over.

The Indianapolis Racers would be dead before I slept again.

"I remember the final moments of the Racers franchise like it was yesterday," fan Randy Greb said in 2004. "On December 15, 1978, TV sports announcer Chet Coppock was on the air all evening with reports from a downtown hotel where there was supposedly an 11th hour savior for the team. But at about 9 p.m. he came on and said, with what appeared to be tears in his eyes, that the team had officially folded. I always think of December 15th as a sad day, even now, all these years later."

Two days earlier, WHA president Howard Baldwin had told the Toronto Globe & Mail, "Indianapolis is like the patient being held together by a machine. When I talked to Nelson, he gave me assurances that he would see out the rest of the year." Skalbania's word was so un-convincing that Baldwin then added, "We will have a contingency schedule (without Indianapolis) ready to go Saturday."

Skalbania, of course, was not present either at the last-ditch negotiations, nor was he in Indianapolis to announce his team's destruction — but many of the players stood by to listen helplessly. "We regret that effective at midnight today, the Indianapolis Racers of the World Hockey Association will cease operations," is how Skalbania's spokesman Gordon Robson told the press. Robson said that Skalbania chose to fold the Racers after the minority partners in the team refused his demand that they both invest more funds and relinquish their rights to settlement money the team might get if the WHA merger with the NHL did not include Indianapolis.

Former player and assistant coach Al Karlander, though critical of the inept management of the later Racers, believes that in August of that year Skalbania intended to complete the 1978-79 season — but that by the time the season started in October he had decided to fold quickly, since all accumulated season ticket money had already been spent.

As expected, Skalbania blamed crippling debts as the cause for the team's demise. He left Indianapolis, not only without refunding the fans' season ticket money, but also with a mountain of unpaid bills in his wake. The Toronto Globe & Mail reported on January 22, 1979 that the Internal Revenue Service seized the Racers' property, citing a $59,000 tax lien. The agency that handled the team's travel also filed a $12,000 suit.

There was also speculation that Skalbania still owned part of the Edmonton Oilers at the same time he owned the Racers — a conspiracy theory given credence by Jack Lautier and Frank Polnasnek in their history of the WHA titled "Same Game, Different Name." They write, "…(Oilers owner Peter) Pocklington secured Skalbania's percentage of shares in the Alberta–based team for $400,000 when the deal (Gretzky sale to Edmonton) was officially made on November 1, 1978."

Skalbania himself contended in Ed Willes' 2004 book, "The Rebel League," that he still owned part of the Oilers, in his statement rebuking Gretzky's contention that the teenager might have gone to Houston rather than Indianapolis. "No, that's not the way I remember it," Skalbania said. "I already owned Indianapolis. I owned half of Edmonton. Why would I want to buy Houston?"

No one will ever be certain if he was at the time a sincere investor, miscalculating wheeler-dealer or shrewd financial vampire — but major league hockey in Indianapolis died in Nelson Skalbania's arms.

LAZY EYES

I earned my first paying job as a journalist at age 18, only a few months after the collapse of the Racers. Writing professionally ever since, I've been lucky to share the sport of hockey I love so dearly. So it might appear in these pages that I have a bit of a chip on my shoulder over the shoddy treatment Indianapolis and its Racers have received since 1979 from reporters who never sat in Market Square Arena themselves.

One of the reasons I wrote this book is to help "set the record straight" about a string of factual errors that I've seen repeated over and over in print since the Racers played their last shift. So let me take the chip off my shoulder and stand on it like a soap box to vent some of my grievances about previous Racers media coverage:

A common assumption repeated since 1979 has been that Indianapolis did not support the Racers. Gretzky's departure from Indy is simply attributed to a failed last-ditch effort by Nelson Skalbania to boost the team's attendance, which has been erroneously reported to be in the range of about 4,000 fans a game. The official Racers attendance for the 1977–78 season (Skalbania's first as owner and before Gretzky) was 7,363 a game, and the average attendance in the brief 1978–79 season with Gretzky was 6,364 a game — both figures admittedly low, but in the same range as the rest of the WHA.

Previously published reports of the franchise's demise also do not note that attendance in Indianapolis averaged just under 10,000 a game — leading the WHA — *before* Skalbania took control of the club, stripped it of its best players and quickly poisoned the relationship the franchise had with its fans. A multitude of plus-10,000-fan games throughout the 1975–77 seasons also proved that Indy would support competitive hockey. Yes, Indiana is basketball crazy, but during that same two-season stretch the Racers' attendance outdrew the professional basketball Pacers by a wide margin — even as the Pacers moved to the NBA in 1976.

Another published report (itself repeated from another unattributed source) claims that Racers' paid attendance figures were inflated, though I have found no evidence of this, and this contention does not jibe with my personal, firsthand recollection of games.

Most stories concerning the WHA and the Racers use simple factual errors as the basis for the contention that Indianapolis was not interested in the team. One book, for instance, makes the curious comment that the Racers failed to capitalize on the public relations boost from a large magazine feature in Sports Illustrated on the Gretzky-Racers signing. It also claims such a piece was perhaps the only place in Indiana that potential fans could read about hockey. That argument is perplexing and inaccurate for two reasons: Indianapolis's two daily newspapers had provided excellent and extensive coverage since the team's 1974 debut — and there was not, in fact, a Sports Illustrated feature published concerning Gretzky's signing with the Racers.

The problem in Indianapolis in 1978 was not the lack of market awareness, the acceptance of pro hockey, or the supposedly blasé Indianapolis fan — it was the fact that the last two years of the Racers franchise was not a good faith effort at putting a competitive product on the ice, and the people of Indianapolis knew it.

It was also obvious to all who read the daily Indianapolis newspapers that buying season tickets for the 1978–79 season was the riskiest of gambles, since the collapse of the team's finances was imminent. The brave season ticket holders who did pony up their hard-earned cash for that ill-fated last season lost their investment after only a handful of home games.

"There is a hockey market here, a fantastic arena and the fans are here. We got 'em. The situation is here. The only thing not here is the money," coach Jacques Demers told the Indianapolis News in June, 1977, shortly before he left for Cincinnati and Nelson Skalbania appeared.

Because Indianapolis was not included in the NHL-WHA merger (and hasn't attracted an NHL team yet), it has been easy for some journalists to simply write off the WHA Racers as an unwanted anomaly in a state obsessed with basketball. This simplistic and inaccurate assumption does not reveal the context of the 1970s franchise's success and failure, its financial and political details, and the motivations of all involved.

No one in Canada would dare contend that former WHA markets Winnipeg or Québec lost their NHL teams because their fans did not care — we all know those teams, as well as the former New England Whalers, were moved simply to make more money. But the blanket assertion that Indianapolis didn't want or care about hockey has been used against the city as a lazy catch-all by those who had never seen firsthand the intensity of a sell-out Racers playoff game. Seeing actual Racers games and knowing the WHA firsthand is key to understanding those tumultuous hockey times. It is important to note that only a few firsthand accounts of the WHA have been published; most books or feature articles are the result of second-hand and third-hand reporting.

And if you were not actually there, you also did not see the human victims of the Racers franchise collapse. Explained booster club officer Judy Stuart in 2006, "France Larose was really pregnant right before the team folded. Her husband, (Racer forward) Claude, had broken ribs. She said that getting out of bed in the morning was the most difficult thing they had to do — Who was going to help whom? That was one of my saddest memories of that last season. How about being very pregnant and finding out your husband was out of a job and had no medical insurance?"

So I do not place the carcass of professional hockey at the doorstep of the Indianapolis sports fan. It lands squarely at the foot of the ramp that leads to Nelson Skalbania's private business jet. While Indianapolis never had an owner with pockets deep enough or long-range plans smart enough to make the Racers an eventual NHL success, it was Skalbania who doomed the franchise.

GHOSTS

SuperFan founder Dave Pickering says it's not an overstatement to say that we had love in our hearts for the Indianapolis Racers. "Here's the thing — I think we still do. In the end it's incredibly painful. To this day, it was one of the lowest feelings I've ever had in my life — when I found out that the team had folded."

The SuperFans faded away along with our beloved Racers. Billy and Dave attended a different high school than I did, so for the rest of my senior year there was no burning reason for us to get back together. We drifted away — and I didn't hear from them for more than 25 years. Our 2004 reunion, just outside Indianapolis, was like climbing into a SuperFans time machine. Complete with new custom-made road-blue Racers uniforms, we looked ready to go — if only the Racers had still been ready, too.

Four WHA teams were absorbed into the NHL for the 1979-80 season: New England, Winnipeg, Québec and Edmonton. The merger worked out pretty well for former Racers Wayne Gretzky and Mark Messier — they would take Edmonton to the height of NHL dominance. They captured a string of Stanley Cups, perfecting the European style of offensive hockey developed by the WHA, and made the game beautiful to behold.

"I don't know where my career would have went if I hadn't gone to the WHA," Gretzky told the Edmonton Sun in 1998. "I'd still have been in juniors. I could have been hurt. I could have got messed up or gone to the NHL in a bad situation. I'm very grateful the WHA was around and that I became a part of it."

But Gretzky's and Messier's ascension into the hockey heavens was bittersweet for Racers fans. We thought we were so close. We fought so hard for major league hockey. We lost.

It's difficult to remember that the Titanic was once a fine cruise ship — right up to the time that it sank, that is. Likewise, because we know the end of the Racers' story — the folding of the franchise in financial defeat — it's difficult to comprehend the time when the organization was a viable, competitive entity, with prospects of longtime success. It might sound silly now, but at the height of the Racers' buzz in Indianapolis, in 1976 or 1977, fans believed the team was on its way to becoming an Indianapolis institution that would last well after our sons and daughters caught the same hockey bug we were enjoying.

At the end of each of the Racers' first four seasons, ending without a WHA championship, the SuperFans would console each other with the literal, "There's always next year" mantra. It always worked — my mind would leap to dreams of the next year's struggle, accomplishment, conflict, drama and opportunity that makes hockey my chosen religion. And we had greater long-range goals for the Racers: We ached for the Racers and the WHA to join the NHL and compete for the Stanley Cup. NHL fans laughed at our boast that one day a WHA team would own "their" Cup.

Yes, there was much work to do before the Racers could silence the snickers. But we knew that as teenagers we had a lot of years left to see the Racers prove them wrong. Or so we thought.

So when "next year" was an impossibility — when major league hockey left Indianapolis seemingly forever — the philosophical lessons were clear to my young psyche. Savor the here and now; tomorrow is not assured. There isn't always next year.

"Think of your own memories of the Racers — they aren't of Messier and Gretzky. Heck, those guys were comets," said booster club officer Judy Stuart in 2006. "It was Ken Block who got carried off with his broken vertebra, but still showed up every night and decided to retire here because he just couldn't see doing any better. Or, 'Mr. Positive Waves' Hugh Harris. Or do you remember Lamey's 'Future Hall of Famer' Pat Stapleton? He didn't quite make it (into the Hall), but do you think he deserved to? Remember how he always made that little ice barrier at the blue line on the power play? How about Reggie Thomas? Not a star, just a hero. Or how about Gene Peacosh? Remember his overtime winner?"

Former Racers fans could watch only minor league hockey in Market Square Arena throughout the 1980s and '90s, which was a difficult pill to swallow after witnessing the Hulls, Howes and Gretzkys of the major league world. I returned to Indy in the early 1980s and sat close to the ice for an Indianapolis Checkers game, in the best seats in the house. But my eyes kept creeping skyward, to my old haunt in the rafters. There were hockey ghost there — my ghosts.

Those teenage ghosts have since been let free, because now there's literally no trace left of the Indianapolis Racers — the venerable old arena was imploded on July 8, 2001. I watched a TV special about its implosion, fascinated and horrified as the building was stripped bare and then blown to bits. Now a plaque memorializing MSA as the site for Elvis Presley's last concert is all that remains.

It might be a stretch for current generations of sports fans in Indianapolis to believe, but at one time Market Square Arena was the positive energy capital of the 1970s pro hockey world. "I've played in a lot of buildings, and when Market Square Arena was rocking, there wasn't a better place to witness a hockey game," former Racer Hugh Harris said in 2006. "Market Square Arena without a doubt was one of the best venues I've ever played in and I've played in the old Montreal Forum, you name it, I've played in it. It was a great arena."

And the erasure of MSA also served as a symbol of the oncoming eradication of pro hockey in Indianapolis. By 2005 Indianapolis stood as the largest North American city without professional hockey of any kind. While the city grew to become the National Basketball Association and National Football League market only dreamed of in the 1970s, it slid back in hockey terms to well before the Racers ever existed.

Nearby Columbus, Ohio now enjoys the NHL team the SuperFans thought should have been in Indianapolis 25 years earlier. Dave Pickering and I took in a Columbus Blue Jackets home game during the 2005-2006 season, with both a sense of joy and melancholy. It took us three decades, but the SuperFans had finally made it to the NHL.

Ironically, just before Dave and I were together again for major league hockey, future Hall of Famer Mark Messier stepped down from the NHL after decades in the game. The former Indianapolis Racer played professionally from 1978 all the way until the 2004-2005 season-long NHL labor lockout. The ironman was the last former WHA player still active when he retired in September 2005.

When Mark Messier waved goodbye to hockey, the Racers' legacy was finally complete.

And now all we have left are dreams of the Indianapolis red, white and blue — and the clicking of skates as the puck falls to ice.

HOME OF THE INDIANAPOLIS RACERS: MARKET SQUARE ARENA

A street-level downtown Indianapolis view of the impressive Market Square Arena, circa 1975 (top), and inside the 16,040 seat sold-out arena during the 1976 WHA playoffs. Even when only half-full, the MSA Racers crowd was boisterous and the noise was deafening by any standards. Racers players and visiting teams alike said they rarely saw the level of affection and devotion exhibited by Indy fans — win or lose.

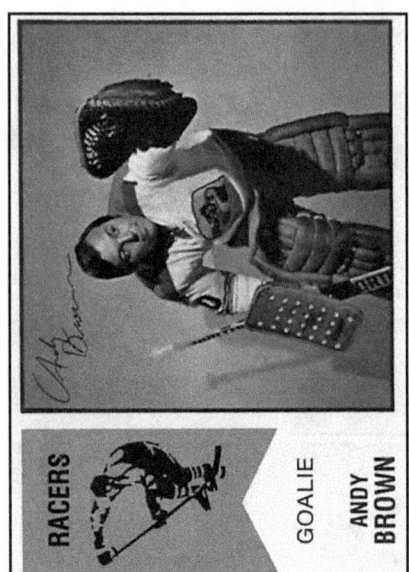

HOCKEY CARDS:
The popular **O-Pee-Chee** sports card company issued **World Hockey Association** cards, including Racers hockey card sets for the team's first four seasons. No WHA cards were issued for the team's final ill-fated season, so a widely circulated **Wayne Gretzky-Racers** hockey card touted as his "1978 pre-NHL rookie card" is a bootleg fake created long after the team's demise.

CLOCKWISE, FROM TOP LEFT: 1974; 1975; 1976; 1977.

Rosaire Paiement (center) gave Racers fans an international Christmas present December 22, 1976 with two third-period goals against the Czechoslovakia national team in Indianapolis. On the Racers bench, (l to r) are **Michel Cairns** (assistant trainer), **Kim Clackson, Dick Proceviat, Ken Block, Jacques Demers** (coach, standing), and **Michel Parizeau.** *(previously unpublished photo)*

courtesy Ken Block

courtesy Jim Park

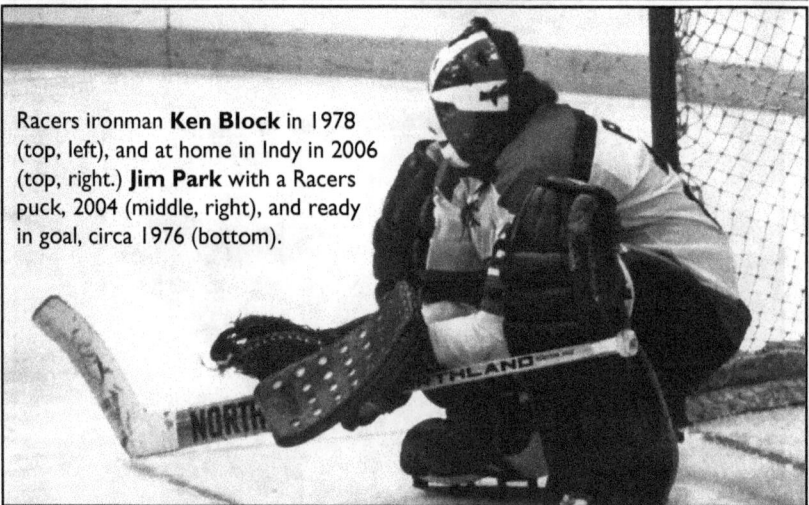

Racers ironman **Ken Block** in 1978 (top, left), and at home in Indy in 2006 (top, right.) **Jim Park** with a Racers puck, 2004 (middle, right), and ready in goal, circa 1976 (bottom).

TOP LEFT: Gary Inness. **TOP RIGHT:** Al Karlander (front) & BJ MacDonald.
BOTTOM LEFT: Gene Peacosh celebrates vs. San Diego. **BOTTOM RIGHT:**
Andy Brown & Kim Clackson. *(Previously unpublished Racers Booster Club photos)*

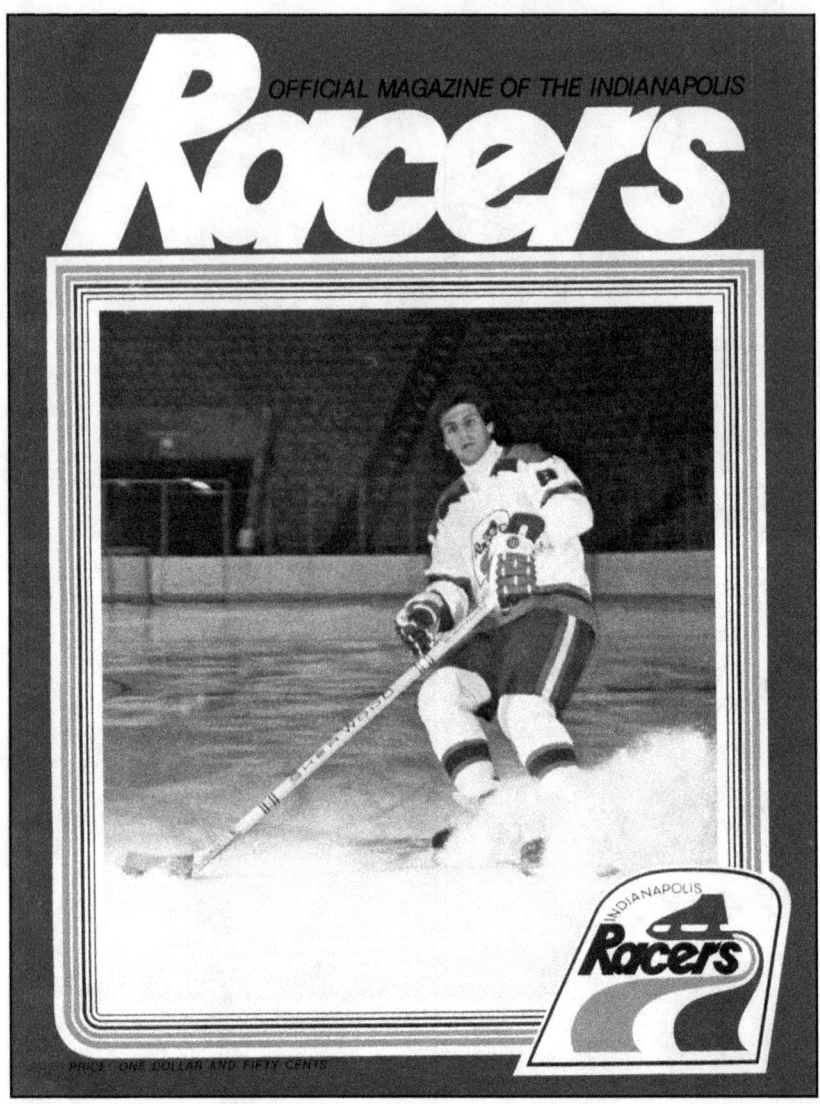

RACERS GAME PROGRAM:

Rene LeClerc was one of the most popular of Racers, pictured here inside Market Square Arena on the cover of a 1977-1978 program.

One of the finest hockey facilities in the world at the time, it is difficult to believe that Market Square Arena was demolished in 2001. Only a plaque remains at the site, commemorating the arena as the last concert venue for Elvis Presley in 1977.

Soon after Elvis left the building, the Racers would also be gone.

RACERS GAME PROGRAM:

Young goaltender **Michel Dion** would blossom with the Racers — even winning the WHA's 1976 Best Goaltender award. Here Dion is captured with a dramatic portrait by artist **Robert Pelkowski** on the cover of a 1976-1977 game program.

Pelkowski's colorful Racers portraits throughout this season created some of the most artistic hockey programs of the 1970s, and are beautiful documents of the most popular players.

WAYNE GRETZKY: The greatest hockey player of all time began his major league career with the Indianapolis Racers. Pictured here in a newly enhanced 1978 team promo photo, Gretzky would soon go on to own every major record in hockey.

With solid ownership, both he and fellow Racer Mark Messier might have brought all those NHL Stanley Cups to Indianapolis — a tantalizing idea that has made the loss of the Racers and major league hockey even more painful for the city.

SWEET SURPRISE: A few legitimate Wayne Gretzky-Racers hockey cards have been issued since the "Great One" developed into hockey's finest player — including this 1982 gem by the Nielson company in Canada, found as a bonus inside a candy bar wrapper.

Considered by many as only a footnote to his career, Gretzky's brief appearance in Indianapolis was vital in forcing the 1979 merger between the NHL and WHA.

MOOSE SIGHTING:

Like "The Great One," **Wayne Gretzky**, Hall of Famer **Mark Messier** got his first taste of professional major league hockey with the Indianapolis Racers. He never wore a home jersey for the Racers — his five-game tryout in November 1978 wearing #18 was on the road.

Messier didn't score a point with the Racers, and finished the 1978-1979 season in Cincinnati, scoring only one goal. The NHL had no inkling of the dominance that Messier would soon bring to that league — but he became the definition of hockey greatness: tough, loyal, talented, determined, a winner. *(enhanced Enor card photo)*

1974-1975 INDIANAPOLIS RACERS

FRONT ROW (left to right): Andy Brown, Jim Johnson, Bob Woytowich, Head Coach Gerry Moore, Bob Sicinski, GM James Browitt, Ken Block, Bob Ash, Ed Dyck. **BACK ROW** (left to right): Equipment Manager Fraser Gleeson, Bob Whitlock, Ken Desjardine, Dick Proceviat, Kerry Bond, John Sheridan, Ron Buchanan, Joe Hardy, Bob Fitchner, Nick Harbaruk, Bill Horton, Jim Wiste, Brian McDonald, Trainer Bill Carroll.

1975-1976 INDIANAPOLIS RACERS Eastern Division Champions Portrait

FRONT ROW (left to right): Leif Holmquist, Dave Keon, Bob Sicinski, Assistant Coach Bob Woytowich, Dick Proceviat, Michel Dion, GM James Browitt, Head Coach Jacques Demers, Captain Ken Block, Jim Park. **MIDDLE ROW** (left to right): Trainer Eddie Swiss, Al Karlander, Michel Parizeau, Kim Clackson, Reg Thomas, Brian McDonald, Renald LeClerc, Blair MacDonald, Francois Rochon, Assistant Trainer Michel Cairns, Equipment Manager Barry Wides. **BACK ROW** (left to right): Nick Harbaruk, Ted Scharf, Mark Lomenda, Darryl Maggs, Bryon Baltimore, Hugh Harris, Kerry Bond, Brian Coates, Pat Stapleton.

1976-1977 INDIANAPOLIS RACERS

FRONT ROW (left to right): Jim Park, Bryon Baltimore, Dick Proceviat, Head Coach Jacques Demers, GM Brian Conacher, Captain Hugh Harris, Michel Parizeau, Michel Dion, Andy Brown. **MIDDLE ROW** (left to right): Rosaire Paiement, Al Karlander, Renald LeClerc, Reg Thomas, Mark Lomenda, Blair MacDonald, Brian McDonald, Bob Sicinski. **BACK ROW** (left to right): Assistant Trainer Michel Cairns, Francois Rochon, Gene Peacosh, Ken Block, Darryl Maggs, Kim Clackson, Pat Stapleton, Equipment Manager Barry Wides, Trainer Eddie Swiss.

1977-1978 INDIANAPOLIS RACERS

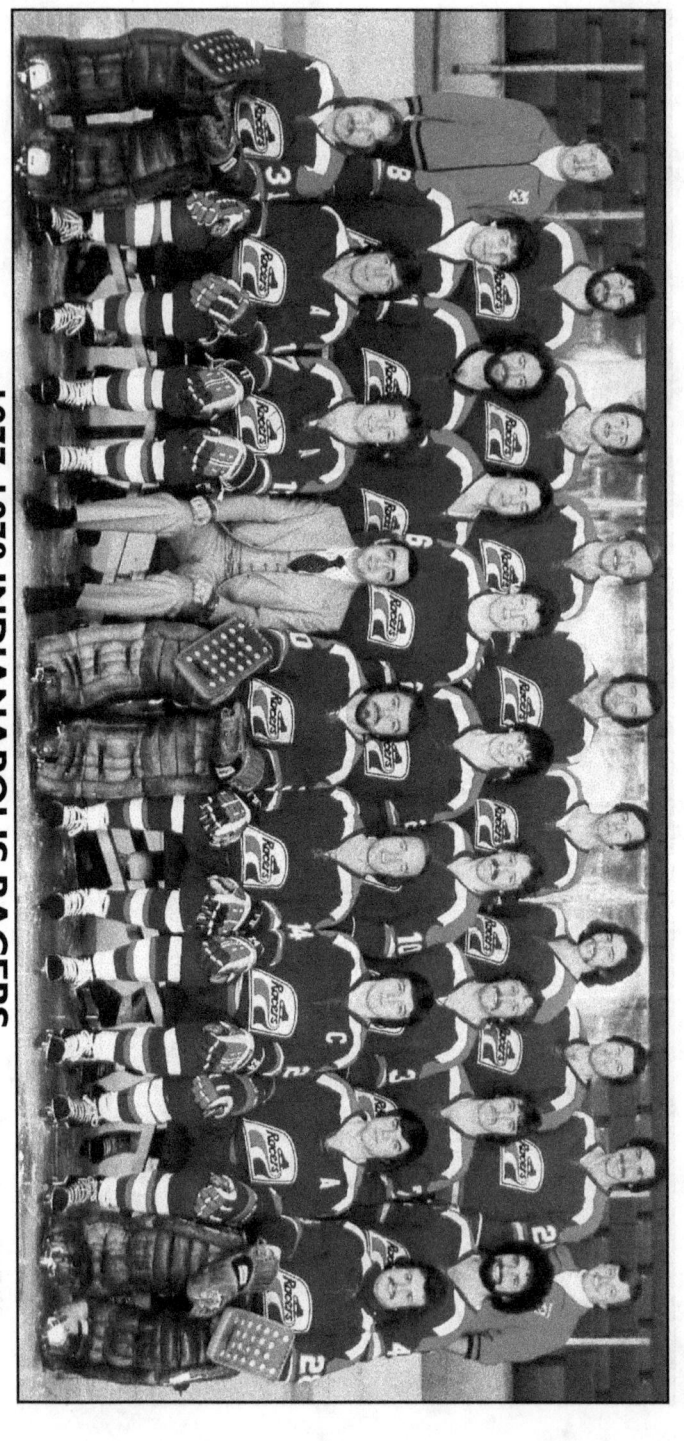

FRONT ROW (left to right): Eddie Mio, Barry Wilkins, Rusty Patenaude, Vice President Don LeRose, Player-Coach Bill Goldsworthy, Captain Ken Block, Rosaire Paiement, Jim Park. **SECOND ROW** (left to right): Ronald LeClerc, Bill Prentice, Peter Driscoll, Charles Constantin, Dave Inkpen, Rich Leduc, Glen Irwin, Blaine Stoughton, Kevin Morrison. **BACK ROW** (left to right): Trainer Bill Carroll, Dave Fortier, Claude Larose, Don Burgess, John French, Michel Parizeau, Kevin Devine, Gilles Marotte, Claude St. Sauveur, Assistant Trainer John Carey.

1978-1979 INDIANAPOLIS RACERS

The **Indianapolis Star** newspaper library confirmed to me in 2005 that this photo was provided by the Racers themselves for the (now defunct) **Indianapolis News** 1978-79 season-preview feature. Notice the large number of skaters — this must have been taken during training camp before a final roster was set. **Wayne Gretzky** sits third from the right on the bottom row — interestingly, a spot usually reserved for team captains or veterans. *(courtesy The Indianapolis Star)*

THE SUPERFANS:

Dave Pickering founded in 1975 the rabid group of teenagers who seemed to live at the top of Market Square Arena for Indianapolis Racers games.

They reunited in Indianapolis in 2004 — more than 25 years after they last saw each other. **Dave Pickering** (#1), **Bill Pickering** (#2) and author **Timothy Gassen** (#99).

(Photo by Sarah Gassen)

RIGHT: the popular 1976 fan button.

INTERVIEW: KEN BLOCK

There is only one Racer player who was on hand to see almost the entire franchise history: Ken Block. From the middle of the first season until the franchise's demise four years later, Ken Block was a Racers constant. Dependable, rugged, handsome, intelligent and friendly, Block would have been an asset to any hockey team in any era. Now a successful businessman in Indianapolis, the former defenseman spoke with Timothy Gassen in 2006.

Timothy Gassen: It seems the connection between Racers players and Indianapolis has been long lasting. What made it a special place for you in your career?

Ken Block: I have the distinction of having worn a Racers uniform for more games (267) than anybody else. They were memorable times, too. I enjoyed the city and enjoyed the people and you know for a couple of those years we had some success and great teammates. When the Racers folded, having been here for about four-and-a-half years and having established some roots, particularly for my children, who were pretty young at the time, it just seemed like a good a place as any for me to try and establish another career and that's why we stayed.

TG: You played one game in the NHL (with Vancouver), but you had a greater opportunity in the WHA. What was your impression of the WHA, since you started out with the New York Raiders?

KB: It gave people like myself an opportunity to really compete at a higher level than the minor league level and to make more money than we were making. It was just an opportunity. I look at it similarly to the rivalry between the American Basketball Association and the National Basketball Association.

In New York, I think the WHA was looked at as an inferior league and even though they were able to attract some of the stars, some of the big names, at least, I'm sure a lot of the players in the NHL thought it was not as good a league — until we started playing each other. I think it took maybe the third or fourth year before they would even agree to play some exhibition games. And the first several years that, as far as the exhibition games went — and maybe it was because the WHA teams were a little bit more motivated to prove that they were as good — they won a fair amount, more than half the games.

I think New York is a tough market and I just don't know the strength of the ownership at the time. I think that financially, that their pockets weren't as deep as some other people in pro sports. That's why the ownership changed in New York. The New York Raiders stayed the entire first year and the second year changed to the New York Golden Blades, but we were only the Golden Blades for maybe a month, month and a half into the season and the ownership fell apart. The league basically felt it important to have a team in that market, so we became the Jersey Knights and played our home games in New Jersey.

TG: As a player, did you think the young WHA would survive?

KB: That never really entered my mind. It think there were some really good franchises in the league, and although over the course of the years there were some that did not succeed, there were new ones that came on. And quite honestly, up until the last day — and maybe I was being a little naïve, not wanting to believe it — but up until the last day, I didn't think the Racers were going to fold.

I just felt that somebody was going to come along or something was going to happen to keep the team going, because for a few years we had one of the best franchises, I felt, in the league. A lot people blame Nelson Skalbania, and I think part of the problem there was that he was a Canadian owner using Canadian dollars to support an American business that just by exchanging the money he was losing 30 percent. I think that had a lot to do with it, but he was no different than anybody else. He was a businessman and looked at a franchise that he was losing a lot of money on, and you know, how long are you going to allow that to happen before you stop the bleeding?

The unfortunate thing is the people who really got hurt are the fans who bought season tickets and never got reimbursed for any of that. That was the real sad thing, I think, that left such a bad taste in a lot of people's mouths about Nelson Skalbania, because it was ironic at the time, he also was an investor in the Oilers franchise. Peter Pocklington was the guy, but Nelson had some of his money in there too.

TG: As a player, did you think that was odd, an owner with interest in more than one team in the same league?

KB: As a player you don't really think about that, all you really think about is performing and winning games. That wasn't anywhere on the top of my mind.

You know, as the captain of the team, I know the years we got to the playoffs in Indianapolis, one of the things we did was we made sure from the playoff games that the gate receipts were turned over and put into the account so we would get paid. But other than that, it just really never — like you said, it's not on the radar screen. You're there really to perform and play.

TG: You came to the Racers half way through their expansion year. There was not a lot of talent in Indianapolis at that time. What was your impression of Coach Gerry Moore and that first-year Racers team?

KB: (laughs) Quite frankly, I don't like saying anything. Somebody told me a long time ago if you don't have anything good to say about somebody…

TG: Would it be fair to say Moore didn't connect well with his team?

KB: The problem was, if you look at the roster changes that first year of the Racers — the first year they were an expansion team — I think there were 80 players who wore the Racers uniform and it's pretty tough to make any connection when that happens.

(Editor: My best estimate is that approximately 40 players were in and out of the Racers lineup during their first year, but an exact number is difficult to document. Block's estimation reflects the perception of a player as he watches the revolving door bringing players in and out.)

Having come here in the middle of the season, one of the reasons that really convinced me to come here was the GM was Jim Browitt. And Browitt was the GM of the New York Raiders my first year in the WHA, so I'd had experience with him and Jim was a fair man and a good man. I had a no-trade clause in my contract. That was the first time in the history of my career that I was traded. I think unfortunately what happens, at least my thinking was, when a player gets traded it's because the team doesn't want you anymore and obviously that's a tough pill to swallow. But Jim Browitt convinced me that sometimes it's because another team really wants you that they trade for you. (So Block agreed to the trade.)

TG: Was Jacques Demers ahead of his time with his coaching management? The old style of bullying players was giving way to the new way of treating players with respect. Society was changing in the 1960s and 1970s — was his approach a reflection of those changes?

KB: That's probably a good analysis of Jacques. He loved the game, understood the game, but as far coaching experience, fundamentally, that wasn't his forte. His forte really was getting the players to play for him, getting the best out of them. He treated us really, really good. We had a lot of fun with him, and he had fun with us. And you could just tell because, quite frankly, there were other teams in the league that had more talent than we did. But as a team we played well together and jelled.

And it took a while. I mean, when we started the year (1975-76), I think four games were on the road. (We) won the first one, ended up losing the three and the very first home game we ended up losing. And that's when Gerry Moore was out and Jacques was in.

TG: Was there a sense of relief on the team that the coaching change had been made?

KB: Well, for me there was. I remember after playing on the road, playing all the games, and when we got home for our opening home game, I wasn't in uniform! (Moore had benched Block after the team's poor start of the 1975-76 season, but he was quickly out of the dog house with Demers' ascension as coach.)

TG: My impression at the time, as a teenager in the stands, was that there was a special bond between players and fans that is not seen usually in professional sports.

KB: It was exactly that way. It was very unique because a lot of teams aren't like that. Today, particularly, it's just such a money business that, you know, I don't think you could get that anymore.

TG: Why would this special bond, this special communication and common sense of purpose, happen in Indianapolis?

KB: God, I don't know. I think a lot of it had to do with the leadership, with Jacques and I think the players that made up the team then, they were all pretty unique — but we were a team on and off the ice. Guys hung together, guys did a lot of things together socially and I think that's important. Where a lot of other teams, it can become a little cliquey, three or four guys go one way and three or four guys go another way — with us it was the opposite, particularly on the road, everybody hung together, everybody went to the same place. Even on your day off, everybody was together, you know. And quite frankly, you spend more time with your teammates than you do with your family during the season.

TG: The very young defenseman Kim Clackson seemed like an energy machine.

KB: Pound for pound he was one of the toughest I've ever played with or against.

TG: Clackson's linemate was Pat Stapleton — opposite playing styles, but it worked.

KB: That pairing was on occasion. When it got down to crunch time, we went with four defensemen: "Maggsy" (Darryl Maggs) and Pat Stapleton played together, Bryon Baltimore and I played together. Kim Clackson, every time he did hit the ice, I think Jacques wanted him to be with Pat because Pat was the most experienced and probably the best-suited to play with Kim. And my partner was Balty (Bryon Baltimore). (Dick) Proceviat would play with "Maggsy" once in a while.

TG: The culmination of the 1975-76 season was your Eastern Division Championship and a classic playoff series with the New England Whalers. The deciding Game Seven was in Indy, with close to 17,000 fans — and we were convinced that you could not lose. But somehow you did. Can you tell us how the team felt at that moment?

KB: Obviously you go through a lot of different emotions first of all. It was disappointing because quite honestly I was convinced and I think a lot of players were convinced we were going to win that game. And the way the game started, they got kind of a freaky goal to start with and then we got down and we were trying to fight back and it just, it never happened. Every time we felt we had an opportunity it was thwarted. But then at the end, it was almost like we let everybody down. It was tough. It was pretty emotional for the players, too.

TG: Every game was like "life and death" in that season.

KB: We used to say, and this was kind of the attitude, "We tricked them again." We tired the other team out in our own end and then we snuck down and scored a goal.

TG: Going into the 1976-77 season, the Racers' team style was in place, you added key players, and goalie Michel Dion continued to play well. It was the apex of the franchise — you swept rival Cincinnati in the playoffs…

KB: And we had to play Québec. We lost to the eventual WHA champs. Looking back, I don't know how many games we won against the Nordiques in the regular season, but it wasn't too many. (The regular season series was six wins for Québec, five for Indy). They had a really explosive team and they had a lot of great players like Marc Tardif and Serge Bernier and J.C. Tremblay, Real Cloutier, they had a star-studded team. They were so explosive. We ended up only winning one game against them in the playoffs, they beat us four games to one and went on to win the AVCO Cup that year.

TG: It seemed that was as far as the Racers could go without adding some really talented players, to match the teams like Québec.

KB: Again, as a player, I don't know how I should say this…as a player I didn't think we needed more players, or that we needed more depth, because players are not responsible for acquiring or trading or whatever. You've got your teammates and you go out and do the best and the chemistry either works or not.

TG: What was it like to see the foundations of the team — Hugh Harris, Pat Stapleton, Michel Dion, Jacques Demers — all leave for Cincinnati, and others with different qualities brought in? As a coach, Ron Ingram seemed to take the opposite approach to Jacques Demers, and you were right back in the basement of the standings.

KB: Tough pill to swallow. You know, I remember the good things. It was tough, because it (the 1977-78 season) was a chore. It was a chore. And again, it seemed like there was a lot of player movement, a lot of changes and to me, whenever that happens, it's tough to establish any stability when every few games you're trading a player or every few weeks you're trading a player and getting somebody else in and changing the lineup.

It's tough to jell as a team and — you know what happens, it's just like anyplace else, when Ron Ingram came in, he wanted to bring some of his people from San Diego. And he did bring in those, and then you've got a new kind of team. You lose the closeness, the team closeness or the team concept that you had before because there are different teammates. I'm not saying anything bad about them, they were obviously also good players in the league, but it makes a team unstable. To me, that was really the last year.

TG: Did you ever have any interaction with new owner Nelson Skalbania?

KB: No, not really.

TG: Were you surprised that Pat Stapleton returned as coach for the 1978-79 season?

KB: When he made a decision to come back, maybe he felt he could turn the franchise around. He may have been told he would have the ability to go get players.

TG: Everyone knew that Indianapolis was not going to be included in a merger with the NHL…

KB: The financial stability of a franchise, that's what was lacking in Indianapolis. The team folded on December 15 (1978), which was supposed to be pay day. I was a player rep for the team for a number of years. And one of the things when we had our meetings, our players' association meetings, one of the things we wanted to make sure we put into the bylaws was if there ever was a merger that players on teams that were not going to be part of the merger, their contracts would get honored.

And the problem with that is that the Racers folded and then there was the merger. So the following year, after the 1978-79 season, four teams merged into the NHL, and the players knew they had this protective clause. But what they did, was they went to the players and said "there's no money here, we'll pay you 50 cents on the dollar, 40 cents on the dollar," or whatever and a lot of players figured, "Heck, half a loaf is better than no loaf at all," and they took whatever the settlement was.

I was one of those who held out and ended up getting 80 percent (of my contact value). Many opted for a lot less than that.

TG: What were you thinking when you heard that a franchise as shaky financially as the Racers was spending more than a million dollars on a 17-year-old kid (Wayne Gretzky)?

KB: Being from Canada, spending my summers in Canada, you hear about this to-be superstar. He was just like a diamond in the rough — when he came here, he was just getting his feet under him. He was never a great skater, but think about it, he's 17 years old, he's developing. He showed signs, you could just see that he was going to, once he gets a little maturity, he was going to be really good.

TG: Was there a lot of talk among the players about the million dollar contract for Gretzky?

KB: First of all, quite honestly, you don't know how it's structured, if it's salary, if it's deferred. There are a lot of things that you don't know about. A lot of people had contracts with deferred income.

TG: For other players, does the Gretzky move make it seem like the franchise can be saved, or it just doesn't make any sense?

KB: To me, what's changed with professional athletes and athletics today compared to back then, a lot of that didn't cross your mind, because you know, you were under contract to play. Players would come and go — Mark Messier played a few road games with us that year, you know. I was a player, and I saw some of this young talent coming in and I was optimistic, that you know, maybe this is going to be good.

Hindsight is always 20/20, but looking back, it's to me the reason the league didn't succeed. They were fortunate to have a merger with at least four teams — but there weren't enough solid owners, the league wasn't strong enough financially to survive.

But back then, as a player you didn't understand it or realize it. Even until the 11th hour, I believed that someone locally was going to come along and say we want to keep the team here, we'll take it over and we'll keep going. But it didn't happen.

I'm a positive thinker.

TG: When the Racers were competitive, people were in the stands.

KB: To me it's the chicken and the egg theory — in order to have people in the stands you have to win games. And in order to win games you have to have the talent on the ice. And if you're not winning, you have to make an investment in acquiring players that can make you a winner.

TG: The attempts to resurrect the team lineup after the 1976-77 season never seemed to work.

KB: When (Bill) Goldsworthy was here, when Don LeRose was the general manager, it was different. It wasn't Jacques, the old guard. Looking back at some of the team photos (from the 1977-1979 seasons), there were a lot of players who had NHL experience. But it wasn't a team that played like a team. There was Claude St. Sauveur, Barry Wilkins, Bill Goldsworthy, people like that. Gilles Marotte, guys like that who'd spent some time in the National Hockey League were on that Racers team, but we didn't play like a team.

TG: How do you think Gretzky handled the start of his pro career? He seemed very nervous the first few games.

KB: Well, toward the end of the year, he started, you could see he was developing. I mean, he's 17 years old playing with grown men, so I think that (being nervous) is human nature. I think anybody that young would feel the same way.

TG: Did you see him then as a budding "superstar?"

KB: Quite honestly, when he played his first few games, he didn't look like one, but he was so young. He showed signs of brilliance. You could just see every once in a while what he could do. I think he has his first goal on tape with Indianapolis, too.

TG: Do you still think fondly of your Racers days?

KB: They were really great memories, especially those two big years in Indianapolis. We had something special here. And I still stay in touch with a lot of the guys. Just last week I talked to Reggie Thomas, Bryon Baltimore and Kim Clackson. But I would hate to leave anyone out — they were all special in their own way.

INTERVIEW: AL KARLANDER

Al Karlander was a rugged forward for the Racers, playing 144 games in Indianapolis from 1975-1977. Like several other former Racers, Karlander made a life in Indianapolis and stayed after the team folded. He spoke with author Timothy Gassen in 2006.

Timothy Gassen: You played for the NHL Detroit Red Wings before jumping to the WHA New England Whalers. As a player, how did you compare the two leagues?

Al Karlander: In the NHL you were playing in bigger venues and bigger crowds and that, but the biggest difference between the competition was really the depth. The top half of the team wasn't a whole lot different relative to skills and abilities. The top half of most of the WHA teams were NHLers, but, you know, it fell off a little bit when you got down on the depth chart. That was probably the biggest difference.

But basically the rules were the same, everything else was the same. It was a lot of fun. You know, you kind of felt like you were trying to sell something and market something, it was refreshing to have some ownership and some management people that were closer to you as far as you were trying to accomplish something, more than just winning a game and trying to get to the playoffs. You were selling a product and they were more supportive with the players as far as making it fun and rewarding and a good experience, but also making it entertaining and making it competitive.

TG: Was there an "us against them" mentality among WHA players toward the NHL?

AK: There may have been for players coming out of the (minor) American league or Central league if it felt like, you know, "I've spent six or eight years in the minors and I can prove that I'm a major league player" — but that wasn't the case with myself.

I actually had been with Detroit for four years. My case was more a situation where Detroit wasn't a lot of fun at that time. It was losing, it had bad ownership, bad management, it just wasn't a fun place to be playing. As strange as that may seem in this day and age, it wasn't a fun environment to be in.

So something fresh and new was also an opportunity. I wanted to see it work, because I was part of it. It was a fresh start, and in Detroit I was what you'd call a utility player. I'd played on any number of lines. I normally played, but I also did penalty killing and specialty type things. And I felt like I was young enough still in my career that I wanted to be a part of the top two lines and the power play and that kind of thing. Detroit was happy with me but didn't see me playing that kind of role going forward.

TG: You had also played with Racer Hugh Harris for New England. What were your impressions of Hughie?

AK: He was a big hockey player at that time. He brought a lot of size. I guess Hughie you look at more as a power forward, and they used him mainly in New England as a wing, and later on here (Indianapolis) at center, and center was a better position for him. But you know the New England team we joined was the defending championship team, we knew there were players there that already had success. We were more coming in to improve the team. They were the best team in the league.

And it was fun to go to a winning team. Boston wasn't the ideal situation because we played in the same facility as the (NHL) Bruins. We weren't the number one hockey team in the community and that was in 1975, with the oil embargo, and there was no fuel. And Boston is a neat city, but it was a difficult year.

Hartford (where the Whalers moved to) I really enjoyed. In fact when I retired from hockey my first choice to settle would have been Hartford, but at that time, 1980, I had a 5 percent mortgage rate here and I would have had an 18 percent there. The economy in the East, Northeast wasn't good. And I did look into that. But Hartford was a great city, I really enjoyed myself there.

TG: You came to Indianapolis after the unsuccessful expansion year, and were part of the team-building and franchise turnaround. What was it like building that Racers team?

AK: We became a team a lot more from just *being* a team than from bringing in all-stars. It really was a team effort, where everybody had a role and everybody played and nobody whined about not having a more expanded role. It just kind of evolved.

(Coach) Jacques Demers is probably the biggest overachiever in all of hockey in what he accomplished, not just here, going on after here. He created a great environment and very basic systems. (He) gave them a lot of freedom and a lot of flexibility in what they were doing or not doing. But he was totally supportive and, like I say, we had some very basic systems and just worked above that. I think a lot of things fell into place.

TG: That defensive combination of veteran Pat "Whitey" Stapleton and rookie Kim "Clacker" Clackson was very interesting — like "fire and ice."

AK: When you're pairing defensemen, that's what you do. You don't want two that are similar. If you've got one that's incredibly skilled you want somebody who will stay at home, too. But Whitey had the smarts to read and react where Clacker was or wasn't, and certainly Clacker gave Whitey a lot of open space out there that just made his game easier. And then anybody who came in, if they fit on the team, you know, they were not only a part of it, they were a contributor to it.

Call it luck, call it what you will, goaltending-wise we had a couple of kids who came in and who played extremely well. On defense we had some old guys. Early on, I think one of the things that gave us some respectability was the toughness. Because even though teams may have won some games early on, when they left the building they knew they'd been in a battle.

TG: My memory is that you made superiorly gifted teams really work.

AK: We felt like this is our building and one of the things that, you know, from a players' standpoint, the enthusiasm of the crowd at Market Square Arena was something that a lot of the players had really not even witnessed before. Maybe not very knowledgeable fans, but fans that cheered us for effort and even though sometimes we didn't get the results we were looking for, they were there every night, they were having fun, and we were in the entertainment business.

We felt good about that, but we also felt we had to give them 60 minutes of hockey and if somebody went away with the two points, they went away with some lumps as well. And we didn't want to make it easy on them. They had to respect our building. And then we won some we weren't supposed to win and just drew on that.

TG: It was a unique situation with the fans, more like a supportive college sports atmosphere than a cold pro sports relationship. It's one of the elements that makes the Indianapolis Racers story unique, I think.

AK: The stage had been set the year before, not only with the losing record but the majority — I shouldn't say majority — but a good part of that team weren't good citizens. And they weren't good in the community to the point where there was actually one place we went after the games that early on there was nobody there and we weren't welcome.

And later on you couldn't get a seat in there because of the positive individuals who were part of the new team. (Before the turnaround) the image of the team off the ice wasn't as good either.

Then there were some characters on the (new) team. Not only did they have a personality, the players that had personality were obvious to the spectators. And with a few without helmets — that's part of hockey that's gone. As far as knowing the personality and character of individual players, it's harder not just with helmets, but with half-shields now, we don't get to see the facial expressions, don't get to see their anger or their joy.

The community just reached out to the players so much and made us feel so welcome and also I think the group of guys that came together were the same kind of guys. There were a lot of good personalities from a lot of different eras and a lot of different teams.

My first year in Indianapolis was the most enjoyable year of my professional career. Not just the winning, just the community and the teammates and the experience. My first year of pro in Detroit was certainly up there with it, but Indianapolis was a unique experience, it was something special.

TG: The next season, 1976-77, was it difficult to keep that positive feeling going?

AK: That year, there were a lot of funny things going on beyond the ice that people weren't aware of. The ownership was so much more supportive early on. I mean money didn't seem to be an issue. I'm sure it always was, but it wasn't that we felt it. Then all of a sudden it became more of an issue after that year.

But also, you know, just the positive atmosphere and the confidence we were playing with was different. You know that next year, all of a sudden you've got a target, and losing to the Whalers (in the 1976 playoffs) was particularly hard for me, because that's the team that I played with the year before and actually got injured with.

That was a hard loss. They beat us at our own game. They beat us by being "loosey-goosey" and wide open — and playoffs are serious and we got too serious on a couple occasions. That's why you win on the road so much, you're looser and relaxed and everybody plays their game more. They came into our building for the seventh game and we were uptight and they just played it easy and we know the results. (A 6-0 Whalers win.)

TG: You said that initially players weren't aware of the team's financial problems. When did it become an issue? Did it stay outside the room?

AK: No, it became a huge issue. Andy Brown's situation, he had a huge contract and late in the year they were trying to jack him around and he stirred up a little bit. But they did a pretty good job of keeping us distant from that.

But the whole general partner group that came in after, they weren't particularly that deep of pockets. But at that point, with hockey in general, teams were cutting their rosters, there were more players than there were jobs all of a sudden and that's why I got out of it. All of a sudden they started cutting your pay and you get a little older and, you know, it hurts a little bit more, and it's going to end at some point so why not end it now?

I had a contract and went to training camp (at the beginning of 1977-78) and said "I just read my contract and I'm not ready to play for this amount, it's just not worth it." And they said "Fine, goodbye." And that was it, and I was willing to make that decision. And that's what happened. In 1978, 1979-80 they were offering players half of what they'd been making the year before because there was just that big a surplus of players out there.

TG: It must have been disappointing to see the Racers slip backward under Ron Ingram.

AK: Ron Ingram, when he came in, that's the training camp I walked out of. Ron Ingram, the things he did when he came in were the beginning of the end. He took that franchise back to where it was the first year and the bar I mentioned to you, again, the players were banned from it. Again, it was the makeup of the team.

TG: You actually came back to the Racers as a coach for the 1978-79 season?

AK: I'd left the year before, but when I came back, Whitey was coach and GM. Whitey asked me to come back, but he wanted me as assistant coach. And then about three to four weeks in, I said, "Whitey, this just sucks, and we're not very good. I think I can help the team, I want to play again." He said fine, so I skated for a few weeks but that's when it (the franchise) ended. I did not dress for a game, but that was kind of the plan, that I'd get back into shape and maybe go into the lineup. But I was assistant coach, plus I had some "Director of Player Personnel" title or something.

TG: Did Pat Stapleton have much management support, that last year as head coach?

AK: Really there was nobody there from previous management to say how to work within the league or outside the league. He (Stapleton) did bring in a couple other people, but it was not well organized. It was overwhelming and you add the money problems to it and it just went in the tank. But why did he do it? I'm only speculating, but Whitey I think said that fall the same thing he said every fall, "I'm just a farmer looking for winter work."

They found him and it was unfortunate because I think under the right circumstances, Whitey could have done a very good job in management or in coaching.

TG: What were your first impressions about Wayne Gretzky?

AK:. When he was here, he was observing. It was another level for him, so he was making some adjustments. Of course, the stats show he didn't light it up the first game or anything like that, but it was obvious that the mental part of his game, that was something that was really special. It was just a question of physically whether he'd grow, what size he'd get to and whether he would stay injury-free.

TG: Did it make sense to sign Gretzky for more than $1 million to such a cash-strapped team?

AK: You know, I was relatively close to the management side of it. I want to say that was probably the worst transaction (team owner Nelson) Skalbania ever made, and I'm sure he's got a list of them. But I'm of the understanding that he sold Gretzky for as little as $50,000.

TG: Could it be that Skalbania always intended to sell Gretzky after a short stay in Indianapolis, knowing that Indy would not be included in the merger with the NHL, but that by signing him he would help force the merger?

AK: I don't think he felt that way in July or August (1978), but I think in September when all of a sudden he realized the entire season ticket revenue was already spent, and then all of a sudden it's October or November and the gate is not covering, the cash flow is not going to cover and he's going to have to write checks for it and he wasn't willing to.

TG: As the 1978-79 season approached, did you think there was the intention to complete that season?

AK: I think there was in August. I don't think there was in October. By that time, after a few home games, what he found financially was enough. I would guess he was given some bad financial statements — I think the season ticket revenue was there to be spent during the year and they spent most of it over the summer.

TG: Why would Skalbania buy the Racers, sign Gretzky, why play that last year after losing so much money? His actions are baffling.

AK: I really don't know whether there was something more from the Edmonton side, and I'm baffled too. How he was going to make it work, I don't know — basically "flipping" was how he made his living. Maybe he felt he could buy the franchise for a dollar with no debt and no liability and could bring in Gretzky and a few others and package this thing and this merger thing, maybe he could flip it and sell it for $2 million and get out of it. And when he didn't get that done, even with Gretzky on board, it was a short-term scheme for him.

TG: What was your impression of the Racers franchise in general?

AK: Initially, the first year I came in on it, it was very well run. Nelson Skalbania, I don't have a lot of hard feelings toward. I think Nelson's biggest mistake is the people he hired as general managers. They knew nothing about hockey and they knew nothing about the community and it wasn't a good fit.

The group before that, Tom Berry and Brian Conacher, they were just up against it financially. The numbers wouldn't work for them and they tried to make them work. Nelson was the last guy standing and he did sell the team out. But the management team he had in place, going into that year, when Nelson folded it, they spent all the season ticket money over the summer. He didn't keep tabs on it or pay attention to it. But Nelson really had no choice. All the money was spent. He made some mistakes and of course he wasn't making it on the other end and he could carry it, but overall the management team that Nelson Skalbania had in place was poor.

TG: This is just conjecture, but if Indianapolis had better management and ownership in place, do you think the NHL would have considered Indianapolis seriously?

AK: I think the NHL would have entertained it more seriously, yes. Do I think it would have been a good thing? No. Indianapolis is not a major league hockey city. There's just not enough of a corporate base here. Not enough major corporations or headquarters or even large regional headquarters. Hockey in Indianapolis, the majority of season ticket holders are going to be families and they can't afford NHL tickets.

TG: So you're not surprised that professional hockey hasn't come back to Indianapolis?

AK: The junior team we have now I think is better than the last pro team we had. But do I think Indianapolis could be a (minor league) American League city? Yes I do. Do I think they should be? Like you say, with the right ownership…

The junior team here is drawing 4,000 to 5,000 a game, which is pretty much the base the (minor league) pro team had. Tickets are a little bit less and, but you know the people still think of it as amateur. It would be like basketball being only freshmen and sophomores. You get some very skilled players, they work harder than the pro league that was here. The minors are not developing the players like they used to. Plus the NHL teams aren't carrying 60 players on a contract like in the old Racer days.

TG: I guess that all makes the Racers' WHA years all the more special. Can you explain the affection the team still generates after all these years?

AK: It really is surprising. I run into people who want to talk about the Racers on a regular basis. … They say, 'I remember the Racers days.' And of course most of them now are your case, went down there as a kid. Used to be I'd run into people who were a hell of a lot older than me that went down there.

The people who are hockey fans in the city, the Racers are still number one in their heart. There are still some youth hockey teams here that go by the name "Racers."

TG: Did you keep any memorabilia from your time with the Racers?

AK: I have an old jersey — but the most notable piece of memorabilia I have is the old skate sharpener. When the team folded we were told, and it was like, "Come on down tomorrow and get your skates and your sticks and clean out your locker." I guess I wasn't thinking that way. By the time I got there, the people who'd been there earlier had cleaned out most of it. The only thing left was the old skate sharpener. So I grabbed it, kind of my last paycheck. I had five children, four boys who played travel hockey, so I got free skate sharpening for 20 years plus — and I still have it.

INTERVIEW: HUGH HARRIS

Outspoken and self-assured, former Racers Captain Hugh Harris stood out throughout his career. He remains one of the most popular Racers, and operates a restaurant on Indianapolis's North Side, not far from the team's old practice facility. He spoke with author Timothy Gassen in 2006.

Timothy Gassen: Can you explain how you ended up in the WHA?

Hugh Harris: I was playing with the Buffalo Sabres, and you didn't want to leave the NHL, every kid wanted to play in the NHL. But when they offered you three times the money to jump leagues, it was really no contest. Money was the number one reason why you left to go to the World Hockey Association. But on my first WHA teams, we only had, I think, one player who — one or two players — who had not played in the NHL, so that was a big factor to go there, because I had friends there.

TG: You spent time in New England, Phoenix and Vancouver in the WHA before ending up in Calgary. But your time in Calgary was not great for you.

HH: Well, I didn't want to go to Calgary. So when I went to Calgary, I was very disgruntled because they were paying all these kids a tremendous amount of money and they weren't even playing. And I just basically refused to play. I sat in the stands.

TG: What made Indianapolis a better opportunity for you? Was it a fresh start?

HH: Exactly. I knew a couple of players on the team, but I knew that they weren't really well coached.

TG: Embracing a positive attitude was important to you to play good hockey. What was the reaction of your Indianapolis teammates when the "Positive Waves" campaign started within the team?

HH: And all that nonsense got started and we had a reporter in town, do you remember Dave Overpeck? Dave Overpeck (of the Indianapolis Star) always wrote his stories with a negative — it always had to be negative. And Dick Denny (of the Indianapolis News) was always positive.

So we started calling Dave Overpeck "Negative Waves" and decided not talk to the son of a bitch, because no matter what you say to him, he's going to turn the story his way. So he would come in and ask somebody a question and he usually would start with me, and I wouldn't even listen to him. Then Dick Denny would come in and I'd talk to Dick Denny. And it got started that way.

TG: Was that "Positive Waves" never-say-die attitude infectious in the locker room?

HH: Well, I think it was in ours, because you know we had a combination of some aging stars, like a Pat Stapleton. We had a lot of guys that had a lot of experience, we had some young kids and I think it was a case where they just kind of blended together.

TG: Players from that turnaround 1975-76 season say that the closeness of the team and the shared attitude that "together you can't lose" was very special. Was it special for you?

HH: I don't think there's any doubt about it because if you go back and look, half the team came from Denver right off the bat (near the beginning of the season). More players came in, like Rene LeClerc and Michel Parizeau from other teams. I came in from Calgary, so basically until the second half of the season, they never really got the team going.

And to really look at it, I think a lot of the players really just wanted to say "Hey, we're good enough to play, we're good enough to be in this league and we're going to show you that we can play."

And I think the best deal was when we swept the Cincinnati team four games to nothing (in the 1976-77 playoffs). They had that big team, it was just experience that beat 'em. They hadn't experienced the playoffs like we had.

TG: How much does Coach Jacques Demers figure into the Racers' turnaround?

HH: I think I'm not a big fan of Jacques. I think he's a great guy to be around, but hockey-wise, most of the players in the dressing room had more hockey experience that Jacques Demers did.

TG: Was he good on a personal level with players, but maybe "Xs and Os" were not his strength?

HH: Definitely. Like I said, he was a great guy, but really and truthfully, even if you look at his stories, even in St. Louis (a later NHL stop for Demers), he seems to be a good coach for a few years until everybody figures him out. The big difference is he is able to get players to play for him. I don't know whether it's a deal where these guys feel they know more than he does, or they actually look at him and say let's try and help this guy out and play a little harder, or if they're playing their own game, where other coaches do not let guys play their own game.

...If you remember Brian McDonald, well, we were sitting at the end of the season, just got beat out by New England (in the 1976 playoffs) and whether it was beer talking or what have you, we were all sitting in this little bar called the Bulldog Lounge and we still talk about this. Brian McDonald said, "You know, we're all going to be out of hockey and that son of a bitch Jacques Demers will probably win the Stanley Cup with the Montreal Canadians in 20 years." And by God if it wasn't 20 years later and that happened. (Demers won the Cup with Montreal in 1993).

TG: He made no bones that that was his eventual goal, which was of course the ultimate goal for anyone in hockey...

HH: Yes, for anybody that played hockey. And no one was sour about it or anything, it was just something that happened, but I consider Jacques Demers one of the luckiest guys in the world, where he got.

TG: Jacques Demers paid you a very high compliment in a 1975-76 newspaper story, saying you were the kind of "money player" that scored the important goals, when the Racers really seemed to need a big goal in a close game.

HH: That was basically the style that they played. If we could keep a team down with the big goals, the players were terrified we would get up on them early, two-nothing, because they knew we'd shut 'em down. But they were also very uncomfortable if they got up two-nothing, because it wasn't going to be safe.

TG: Talk about your personal attitude of always working, always staying positive in tough games.

HH: It seemed to come that way, but I think it started so small, that "Positive Waves" deal. You know I can remember Gordie Roberts in New England one time, he'd scored a goal and it made it two-nothing and our players just stood up and said, "You son of a bitch you better score another one!" and I think we beat 'em like 5-2 in their building, and that's just the way it was. We really didn't care who scored the goal, but someone got their ass in there and scored a goal and that seemed to be the way it was.

TG: After the 1976-77 season, much of the Racers backbone left for Cincinnati, but you stayed until a trade later the next season. What was that like?

HH: That was the time Ron Ingram took over, and you talk about an idiot, this guy, no one knew where this guy was coming from. It was almost like he was an ex-player with a grudge. He seemed to have the mentality, "My god, I played for only $5,000 and you guys should be doing the same thing." I don't know how, why, where or what that guy was thinking about, but he was probably one of the most two-faced characters I've ever run across. I think the guy's dead — I have no sorrow for that. He was the type of a guy you just couldn't trust. Jacques Demers you could trust with your life. This guy, you know, you couldn't turn your back on him because he was a liar.

I was traded along with Bryon Baltimore, for Richie Leduc and Blaine Stoughton who was their top player. Stoughton would go on to score 50 goals in the National Hockey League. Richie Leduc was one of the better players.

TG: Many of the most important Racers were with the Stingers in 1977-78, but the result there was disastrous. What happened?

HH: We had Michel Dion and Mike Liut as our goaltenders. It was kind of funny. The next season, those guys were playing at the NHL all-star game, but that year in Cincinnati neither one of them could stop a beach ball.

TG: How aware were you of the chronic financial troubles with the Racers?

HH: The team was supposed to take a pay cut to keep the franchise going (in the 1976-77 season). Well, I voted against that and I actually threw all the paychecks in the garbage. And you have never seen such a fight in the garbage can as the guys were grabbing paychecks. But I refused to take it, because Pat Stapleton and I could have gone to the (NHL) Chicago Blackhawks. Some of the guys signed waivers but I would not sign a waiver on my contract because the minute they didn't pay me, I was a free agent. And at that time I could have gone to about damn near any team in the league.

At that time it was about seven to eight weeks before the trade deadline and Pat came up to me and he said, "Listen we can both go to Chicago tomorrow if we want to." Pat's word was good for me. I could have gone to Québec, there was a bunch of things going on at that time. And things were going real good.

TG: Are you surprised that people remember that Racers team?

HH: Oh, I think they remember it because you always remember good times. And I think a lot of the people remember going to the games. We used to go to the (American Basketball Association) Pacers games and there was nobody there and I couldn't figure it out, I said, "What the hell is going on here?" And you'd come to our games, and it was alive.

I think the people didn't know a lot about hockey, but I think they realized what effort was. And I think when they'd seen some aging stars come in — even though Bobby Hull was a great player, he was an older player and he had the two Swedes working for him. You know, Gordie Howe would come in, he was a name, but he put out a good effort. He may not have been the Gordie Howe of years ago, but shit, anybody would have taken him on his team. So there were a lot of players like that. So I think the people realized that they were getting their money's worth.

TG: Are you surprised that Indianapolis has no professional hockey?

HH: I am, I really am. I can't figure it out. I believe Indianapolis would be a heck of a city with a minor league American Hockey League team. And then build — get your front offices and everything into place. I was in Nashville and witnessed an NHL game there. Now if Nashville, Tennessee can pack 'em in, I can't believe that Indianapolis can't do the same thing.

You can remember, as I can remember, them announcing in Market Square Arena at a Racers game that is it was going to be held up a half an hour because there were too many people standing outside in line to get in. So if that can happen once, that can happen twice. And I think it's a case of Indianapolis getting serious with some money.

TG: Do you think your teammates would agree that it was special in Indianapolis in the 1970s?

HH: I would just say that probably for the players that played in Indianapolis at that time, it was the best time of their life in a hockey situation. And also with the fans, because the players were very accessible to the fans, and I don't think there was ever a place that I played that the fans were so generous. Even in defeat, you wouldn't get booed off the ice.

I think the fans caught on to the "Positive Waves" idea. I can remember many a night going out there and saying, "Oh my god they're fired up tonight." That would obviously not only fire us up but put a little fear in the players that were coming on the ice at the other end. It was a loud building!

TG: Have you kept much memorabilia of your Racers days?

HH: I was never a collector — but before the 1977 WHA All-Star Game (with Harris in the lineup) I went up to Gordie Howe and Bobby Hull and I said, "If you guys wouldn't mind, I would love to have a picture with both of you guys, because I'll probably never be on the ice with you two again," and they said sure — and a lady, a photographer took the picture.

Well the goddamn All-Star game started about 30 minutes late because every player — outside the guys who were big-shots themselves — then got in line to have a picture, too, and right after the national anthem Gordie Howe comes up to me and says "You son of a bitch!" (laughter)

INTERVIEW: JIM PARK

Jim Park is one of the perfect former Racers to discuss the team's rise and fall, joining the franchise after the first team camp in 1974 and playing through the 1977-78 season. He and fellow Racers goaltender Michel Dion were sent together to the minor league Mohawk Valley Comets of the North American Hockey League, and would both come back up in 1975 to help bring the Racers franchise to its greatest moments. Park battled on, through injury and a revolving door of other Racers goaltenders and was released only before the team's last partial season — though his career in Indianapolis was not over, as you will see. Now the head of the Jim Park Goalie School near Toronto, Park has both a son and daughter playing his position: goaltender. Jim Park talked with author Timothy Gassen in December 2004.

Timothy Gassen: You spent the 1974-75 season at Mohawk Valley getting ready for major league hockey. What was that experience like?

Jim Park: It was the minor team for both the Racers and (WHA) Toronto Toros, and it was a lot of fun. It was a wild experience, because that was the "Slapshot" league. (The NAHL was used as a basis for the 1977 comedy film "Slapshot.") There was always wild stuff going on — they called it a "hatchet league" — and if they looked at it today they would say we were all insane. That was the time of the (Philadelphia Flyers') "Broad Street Bullies," that's the way the game was played. That was also the time of bench clearing brawls and all that.

I didn't look at it as a punitive experience. I was still very young, and I was looking forward to the opportunity and developing for what was to come. You have to have patience and believe in your ability and develop a positive attitude — that's how you get to the big leagues.

TG: Can you describe your role during the Racers' heroic rise to Eastern Division Champions the next year, 1975-76? (Park recorded two playoff shut outs, too.)

JP: I was only up for the last couple of months of the season. Actually, I had been released by the Racers — there was a bunch of contracts they released, and I signed on to stay with Mohawk Valley — then Andy Brown hurt his back. So then I had an opportunity — because they needed me — and I wanted to go back up and show them that they were wrong to release me in the first place.

TG: All players compete for ice time — what was your relationship with the other goaltenders on the club?

JP: Michel Dion and I had already played together for a few years, so we were already friends. We always competed with each other, pushing each other — we both wanted to play, but we were friends and we wanted each of us to be successful. I was lucky, I got along with all the goalies that I played with.

TG: In 1976-77 you played the second most games for a Racers goalie (31), winning 14. Why did the team acquire new goalie Paul Hoganson?

JP: I had injury problems toward the end of the year, so I think that's why Paul Hoganson was brought in. And that's what happened when you get hurt, it can be hard to get back in the lineup, and we got in the playoffs and "Hoagie" got hot. He came over from Cincinnati, so he wanted to show them what he could do when we faced them in the playoffs.

TG: Even though the team had played wonderfully in the 1977 playoffs, was there a feeling on the team that you should have gone further?

JP: You always want to believe you can go further. But that was a tough Québec team with a lot of talent, so it's hard to say you should have won a series when you go down four games to one!

TG: In 1977-78, with new coach Ron Ingram, you only play 12 games, splitting time with Ed Mio, Gary Inness and also Peter McDuffe. Why was there less opportunity for you?

JP: Ron Ingram and I never got along, I can tell you that. Gary Inness was going to be his guy, and I wasn't. He was brought in from the NHL to be the #1 guy, and Eddie Mio, too, so that's the way it is with goalies. It was just a big mess.

I played the very last game of the year, and I remember that the guys didn't want to win that last home game because it would put Cincinnati into the playoffs. (Indianapolis was in last place, but Cincinnati and Birmingham were dueling for the last playoff spot. The 9-7 win by Birmingham at Indy secured the last playoff spot for the Bulls instead of the Stingers.) You can tell your time with a team was coming to a close at that point, and I wasn't getting played.

TG: Even though you had left the team, were you suspicious about the whole Skalbania and Gretzky affair in Indianapolis?

JP: It never made any sense to me! There's a whole conspiracy story there, and that never gets any play, I never hear people talking about it!

TG: After the Racers, you played in the Pacific Hockey League for Los Angeles and Phoenix in 1978-79, then — surprise — you're back in Indianapolis with the minor league Checkers from 1979-1981. What was that like for you to return?

JP: It was great. There were still great fans there, and it was a very enjoyable time, absolutely. I thought after that I might get another break in the majors.

TG: Then you play a career-high 53 games for Fort Wayne in the International Hockey League for the 1981-82 season…

JP: I ended up signing back with the (NHL) New York Islanders, but you have to look at who is in front of you (in the organization), and there wasn't a lot of opportunity for me at that point. I wanted to play for 10 years, and that last year in Fort Wayne was my 10th year.

TG: Are you surprised that a city the size of Indianapolis now has no professional hockey?

JP: I really am surprised that Indianapolis doesn't have a pro hockey team. I always felt it was a good hockey town. Market Square Arena was a wonderful place to play and had a wonderful atmosphere, all the sound stayed in the building and the sightlines were great — they don't have that now with the old Fairgrounds arena.

TG: Was your experience with the Racers satisfying?

JP: It sure was but it would have been great if it lasted longer! But during that playoff run you couldn't ask for anything more exciting. The town was behind us, we had great fans, and the yelling and screaming they would do would make your hair stand up on the back of your neck sometimes. It taught me a lot about what a team is all about, because that truly was a team and we couldn't have achieved success any other way.

TG: Are you also surprised that the Racers are still remembered so fondly all these years later?

JP: Yes, I suppose it's surprising, but I can remember times following the Maple Leafs when I was young, and they seem like yesterday. So I can understand it. It's a magic time when you're young like that, and it was a new game that was brought to town, so the fans were learning a great new game from Canada brought to basketball country.

TG: The WHA is finally starting to get some well-earned respect…

JP: You have voices speaking up for the WHA now, players and people who were involved in the WHA speaking very highly about how competitive and exciting the WHA was. And that goes against what the NHL would have liked you to believe back then, and even now they still won't let their grudge go. But it was an exciting time, especially in Indianapolis.

INTERVIEW: ED MIO

Ed Mio has gone on to a 30-year career associated with professional hockey, but in late 1977 he was just beginning to show his goaltending talent — with the Indianapolis Racers. He talked with author Timothy Gassen in 2006.

Timothy Gassen: Before Birmingham, you also played in the WHA with the Calgary Cowboys?

Ed Mio: I was signed with Calgary and played only three games. I was called up when (Don) "Smokey" McLeod was hurt. They had Gary Bromley — had they not had Gary Bromley in the off season, I probably would have been the goaltender there. They sent me down to the minors.

When Calgary folded, Birmingham picked me up and again I was the third guy there because of Wayne Wood and John Garrett, but I did play a little bit there and that's where I got my opportunity, because I played well in the minors, and Indianapolis needed a goaltender. So I didn't play a lot in Birmingham, even though I was up there, half and half, but I didn't have a lot of games with Calgary and Birmingham.

TG: What was the goaltending situation and team atmosphere like when you came to the Racers in the 1977-78 season?

EM: I was brought in, in late '77, on loan from Birmingham because I think Gary Inness went down and they didn't have any goaltenders. So I was on loan, supposed to go back to Birmingham in '78. It turned out they (the Racers) wanted to keep me, so they made a deal with Birmingham. In '77 I didn't know about it, I just thought I was on loan and that's the way they operated back then in the WHA. I guess in that summer of '78 after the season was over they completed a deal to keep me.

First of all, the atmosphere when I got there was, I was playing so the other guy wasn't and I think it was — can't remember if it was me and Jim Park or Gary Inness — but they needed another goaltender, that's all I remember. So there wasn't an atmosphere that somebody was in there trying to steal their jobs, it was just they needed two goaltenders and I was the second at that time and I just happened to play well and I guess they wanted to keep me.

We went back in '78, that's when we had four goaltenders: Gary Smith, Gary Inness, Jim Park and myself. And I guess the writing was on the wall for Gary (Smith) and Jim Park, but we alternated three goaltenders for the first two weeks or whatever it was. And we all seemed to get along. The guy who was really on the way out was Jim Park. But we all seemed to get along. Jim was a great guy, understood his situation, probably knew he was the fourth guy.

Gary Smith, coming in with NHL experience, perhaps we all thought he might have been the guy they wanted to bring in. But it turned out that I still played. It was me and Gary Smith actually, but I remember there was a time where Gary Inness would just make the road trips. So if I was playing the game, whether it was in Québec or wherever and the next game was at home, whoever was scheduled to play that game would stay home, so Gary (Smith) would be the backup or Jim Park would come on the road trips.

Then when we went back home, it depended where our next game was, whether I went on the road ahead of time, you know what I'm saying. It wasn't a bad atmosphere, we all got along. Gary Smith was a great guy and "Inch" (Gary Inness), he was good, in a quiet kind of a way. But again, in the WHA, it seemed if you were older and weren't in the NHL anymore, that was probably your last stepping stone to retirement.

TG: When you came to the Racers, Ron Ingram has already been let go, and former NHL star Bill Goldsworthy was then player-coach. What was the team makeup like?

EM: We had a lot of veteran guys. The other guys who were still in Indy — Kenny Block, Rene LeClerc, Blaine Stoughton — we had a pretty good group of guys. It was just playing wise, we were a little behind. So I can remember our dressing room atmosphere was good. I think we were in last place, and we just went out and played hard every night. We still had a pretty good nucleus of fans, around 8,000 or 9,000 coming, and we got along great and Bill did a pretty good job.

We had a lot of veteran guys, with this longtime NHL French defensemen who came from Cincinnati (Gilles Marotte) — he was great in the dressing room.

Going into the summer, Bill (Goldsworthy) decided to play again, so he went back to Edmonton, and Pat Stapleton took over and we were starting off pretty good, the 1978-79 season.

TG: As that last 1978-79 season approached, what was the reaction of the guys to the signing of this 17-year-old prospect, Wayne Gretzky?

EM: Again, he was 17 years old. So I don't think anybody thought that he was going to come in and just set everything on fire. But it was a good start for a franchise — again, I think we were in last place — and people were excited, the city I think was excited that they were getting one of the best young prospects to come out of Canada. There was a lot of excitement and especially that first week of skating, I know there were a lot of people coming out just to see Wayne.

But we did think we had enough guys that we would have a better year, starting fresh, a new coach, an experienced coach, a guy that knew. So the excitement was there for the players, as it is for every team that starts out in late August and September. But I don't think the excitement was there that Wayne was going to lead us to first place.

TG: Was the thought of merger with the NHL at the front of players' minds as you started that 1978-'79 season?

EM: No, you know what, we always knew the WHA was starting to head into some problems. So I think for myself, personally, it wasn't until I got to Edmonton that I started thinking that the merger was going to happen, because Edmonton was strong, it was a Canadian city, they had supposedly some money behind them. So I felt really good that if there was a merger, I was in a good spot. And I think talking with Wayne and Peter Driscoll they'd tell you the same thing, that once we got to Edmonton, there was a lot of things for us that made it more relaxing to know we were in an established place. That if there was a merger, we thought we were one of the teams that was gonna go.

And at the same time, leaving Indianapolis, we still heard rumblings that they were about to fold, and Cincinnati wasn't strong, either. So we felt really good there (in Edmonton). When I was in Indianapolis I don't think any of the guys felt good about Indianapolis being one of the teams to be accepted in the merger and as it turned out, a month after, they folded.

TG: So you weren't surprised come December 1978 when the Racers folded up their tent?

EM: I can't say that I was surprised, but I wasn't too worried about it anymore because I was in Edmonton, I was in a good place. We didn't want anybody to fold, because you know, hey, you fold now it makes it six teams and if Indy folds we figured Cincinnati wasn't too far behind so now we'd only have five teams.

TG: Bill Goldsworthy said later that he recommended to Edmonton to buy the three of you — Wayne, Peter Driscoll and yourself — from Indianapolis.

EM: I think that Bill, when he went to Edmonton, with his relationship with Glen Sather, he obviously put in a good word. He got to know us pretty well personally and coaching us the last three months, four months of the (previous) season. So I have no doubt that Bill had something to do with placing in Glen Sather's mind about Peter and myself. I'd have to honestly say that was definitely in the making.

TG: You are one of the few hockey people who have seen Wayne Gretzky ever since his first days as a pro. Can you tell us what it was like to watch his progression into the most important player of all time?

EM: I don't think he was ever a 17-year-old kid. I mean, he was mature beyond his years. Again, when we got there, he lived with a family, he was hanging around with a lot of people his own age, but in the dressing room, yeah, you could see the tenacity and the fortitude that he had of wanting to be one of the best.

He didn't come along right away in Edmonton. It wasn't until late January that he started blossoming into the player he really is and will be remembered as. But it was something I'll always be able to have as a memory, of being there right from the start with Wayne and right to the end, and now working with him (as part of the NHL Phoenix Coyotes).

You just saw, and I hate saying "greatness," but you just saw everything with this young man. It just kept getting better every year. Unfortunately I was traded (from Edmonton) halfway through '81 and that's when Wayne really took off. I think in late '81 he started becoming the leader and that part I wasn't privileged to see.

Again, I got to see it and still played against him, and still carried on a pretty good relationship with him. I am grateful, and you can see the signs and how everybody just kind of flocked around him. It was good, it was nice.

TG: You had a long and fruitful career in the NHL. Was there an attitude that the former WHA players had something to prove to the NHL veterans?

EM: I don't think it was that at all. I think hockey players respect what you do. It's got nothing to do with the fact that you came from the WHA, because there were a lot of guys that left the NHL to play in the WHA. I think in any league that you play — AHL, East Coast — hockey players have a respect for what you can do. So if an East Coast kid came up and played on the American Hockey League, I don't think the team he's playing for would look at him like, "Oh, you were just in the East Coast League."

And I know is we never ran into it. It's hard for me to explain there, because most of our team came from Edmonton, which were all (former) WHA guys.

TG: Do you think that some longtime NHL business people only downplayed the quality of play in the WHA for self-interested business reasons?

EM: That's all it was, it was all business, it was competition for them. But you gotta remember, if you look back at '72, how many NHLers jumped ship. Then in '77 I think it was, '76-'77, they started taking the 18-year-olds because the NHL still had their 20-year-old draft, and the WHA was offering the (big) money.

Now there was probably animosity at that time because you know they (WHA) were taking a loophole, and they did have a draft but they could make it 18-year-olds. Like I said, if it wasn't for the NHLers there wouldn't have been a WHA league. Again, it's a pro league and it's somebody playing a sport that they love, and I think there's respect for that.

TG: No serious hockey person is going to convince me that the WHA Winnipeg Jets were not one of the greatest professional teams of all time…

EM: With the Europeans coming over, there was no animosity within the WHA. No animosity saying, "Oh you only played in Europe." There's good hockey in Europe and we're seeing it now. Again, there's no animosity now in the last 10 years that the Europeans started flooding the market. It's now about the best players in the world being able to play.

TG: Has the WHA left a positive legacy to help change pro hockey?

EM: You gotta remember some of it was also considered goon hockey back then too. But I think the overtime rule, just the certain small changes to the game (did help). I think the legacy perhaps could be that the WHA opened up different markets that the NHL decided to later open up, too. That legacy has proved that hockey should survive although we're still struggling in the Southern states and sometimes in Phoenix.

It allowed a lot of different guys to play the game that might have been overlooked in the NHL. It just opened up the eyes (of hockey people), and perhaps the NHL took more of a scouting approach. You know organizations now have scouts everywhere and I think perhaps in the '80s that's when the NHL said, "Look it, there's a lot of hockey players out there, we'd better fortify our staff and get out there and watch, because the WHA had some hockey players that we overlooked."

TG: Is it fair to say that the WHA's solid teams, the Edmontons, the New Englands, they belonged in the NHL all along?

EM: I think so. I mean Edmonton won four Stanley Cups with Wayne and they were still kind of a WHA backbone, most of the guys who played in '78-'79. Granted, they built it through the draft also — Glenn Anderson, Kevin Lowe, they weren't WHA players, Paul Coffey and all that. But it allowed Edmonton to show their stuff, see what kind of city it was, you know things like that.

TG: I think Edmonton's transition to the NHL is amazing, considering how the NHL did their best to strip the former WHA teams of important talent.

EM: We made the playoffs our first year in the NHL. We had the majority of our team from '78 — Glen Sather did a great job. We were all supposed to go back to our teams that drafted us in the NHL, but he was able to make deals with these teams to keep our players, like Ron Chipperfield, myself, the majority of our guys in '78 stayed at least to the '80s and then Glen was able, with his staff, to build it through the draft and they did an excellent job.

Obviously Mark Messier helped coming over from Cincinnati (of the WHA), so they did a great job through the draft and their scouting staff was excellent. So they built it the right way, as did Winnipeg.

Winnipeg was able to keep most of their WHA players and they had pretty much good success. It was just Hartford and Québec didn't have the success, but then Québec built it through the draft.

TG: Indianapolis now has no professional hockey. Is that surprising to you?

EM: It is. I loved Indianapolis. I thought it was a great town, great place to live, great people, fan support, the base of it was great. It is a shame in a way but again I'm not qualified to tell you why no one has even looked there. But yet they've had minor league hockey that seemed to go for a little bit, and then didn't. So that has to have something to do with it. You gotta go places where there's success.

TG: Finally, you are now (2007) the Director of Player Development for the Phoenix Coyotes. What are your duties for them, day to day? *(Editor's Note: Mio has since left this position.)*

EM: My job is to work with all our draft pick prospects and a little bit with the minor league team once they're first or second year pros and what I would do, I go in, watch them play, not only for one night, go in for a couple games, three games. I might spend three or four days with the individual and write reports for myself, try and help the individual, almost like another coach without being their coach, because the coaches don't like that.

And try and carry on contact with the individuals to know that we're interested, explain, "This is where you've gotta get to, to be a Phoenix Coyote," and carry on a one-to-one where our scouts can't do that and stay after a game and talk to the individual. And at the end of it, at the end of their junior career or college career or whatever, I make recommendations whether we should sign them, this is where I think this person is going to end up, where he's going to play, or will he ever play. So it's a day to day job with the prospects.

TG: In 1977, playing for the Racers, could you have imagined that 30 years later you would be in management in the NHL?

EM: No, I was hoping to play a little bit more so I could make more money and wouldn't have to work. (laughter) I mean, it is a job, it's a paycheck, but more importantly it's a job that you love. You love waking up and knowing that, "Hey, I'm working for an NHL team!" And I think people are very lucky to find two things in their lifetime that they enjoy, and actually I found three because I was an agent for 10 years and had a very nice clientele list. So for 10 years doing that with Mike Barnett, actually him and Wayne brought me into the business then, too. And I don't think you can go down the list in our population and find three different careers that you all love what you did. And still be here to enjoy it.

INTERVIEW: SUPERFAN DAVE PICKERING

Dave Pickering was the captain of the crazy teenagers who lived at the top of Market Square Arena for Racers games and called themselves the SuperFans. Along with his younger brother Bill Pickering and author Timothy Gassen, the SuperFans were devoted to the Indianapolis Racers — and in memory they still are. After years of searching, Gassen finally found his fellow SuperFan Dave Pickering, still living in Indianapolis. He talked with Pickering in August 2004 about the SuperFans legacy.

Timothy Gassen: How did the "Rafter Rats" (fans at the top of Market Square Arena) inspire you to start the SuperFans as a teenager?

Dave Pickering: I saw games in the first season and thought it was so exciting, then early in the second season I met the Rafter Rats.

I told my mom and brother Bill that I wanted to do that, too. I was 16 at the time, Billy was 14. I wanted my own identity, and came up with the SuperFan. So I had my Mom make me a red cape, and I had the Superman "S" put on and the name "SuperFan" in letters underneath. I started to wear it to games, and everyone seemed to like it.

Then I came on the idea to use plastic cushions to whack on concrete to make noise. I was whacking the step on the top of the arena and it got the crowd going, but that first cushion only lasted one game!

TG: Then the banners started coming…

DP: I started making banners out of bed sheets and Magic Markers — a lot of Magic Markers. After the big SuperFans banner (about 6 feet high by 15 feet wide that hung on the arena wall), came the referee eye chart that spelled out "A BAD CALL BY THE REFEREE." Another was a double-sided banner — one side said "Great Shot" for a Racers goal, and "Lucky Shot" for an opposing team goal. I had at least a half dozen banners for each game.

TG: The SuperFans were as far away from the ice as possible…

DP: I deliberately picked that spot so we wouldn't be annoying the crowd with our antics. We could spread out and take up a whole row at the top. But for sell-outs or near sell-outs, we were suddenly pushed together. But the people who had been there knew us and knew we were there for fun and that we were supporting the Racers.

TG: So how did I get sucked into the SuperFans?

DP: We had a bugle and other stuff to make noise, a cow bell, and all kinds of extra stuff. You came up to see what we were doing and we let you hang out with us. Pretty soon you were joining in, making noise with some of our extra stuff, and that's how you joined up.

TG: I remember that I had a garbage can lid and a drumstick! That must have been quite a sight for everyone — to see you, Billy and me at the top of the arena with all of our stuff making all that awful noise and carrying on...

DP: Absolutely insane!

TG: I don't seem to remember that we were really mean-spirited about the other teams, we were more positive than that. Maybe if we had been a little older, it would have been different.

DP: Exactly. We were about cheering for our guys. Sure, we'd make cracks about how old Gordie (Howe) was, stuff like that, but all in fun.

TG: I remember that there was a referee named Ron Ego, and that was a great name for fans like us to have fun with. Do you remember how Channel 13 sportscaster Pete Liebengood made fun of us on TV?

DP: Oh yeah, we were not happy about that, so we made a banner — it read "Liebenbad." (laughs)

TG: But most of our banners were really positive...

DP: Like the one for Bill Goldsworthy (who joined the team in the middle of the 1977-78 season). He was a great player in the NHL, and we looked up his stats. We only had two days to do something after it was announced he was coming to the team, and we worked night and day to make a huge banner that read "Goalsworthy." We told him after the game that we made the banner, and he was really nice about it.

TG: We'd go down to meet the players after almost every home game...

DP: The players got to the point that they knew us by sight – I'd still be wearing the cape, and they were all really nice. Bill was great at getting autographs with all of them, and he still has a lot of autographed programs.

TG: What did we think when we were featured in a game program (in the 1977-78 season)?

DP: We thought it was so cool! We were in an actual program! How often does a normal fan get featured in a pro team program? Now, we weren't your "normal" fans...(laughs). We were the nuttiest fans, and the crowd would wait for us to lead them. On the road, that's what we would do, too — lead the procession around the arena.

TG: Maybe on the road the older Racers fans just wanted us to be the targets.

DP: Yeah, maybe the crowd would run out of trash and beer bottles after they got through with us! (laughs)

TG: It sounds like the SuperFans was a big thing for us as teenagers.

DP: This was *the* thing for us to do in our high school years. It sounds tame by today's standards. We'd talk all the time about the team, talking about trades, talking with the booster club about other game scores, that sort of stuff. All hockey — all the time!

TG: But the 1978-79 team was awful…

DP: They had lost everything — scoring, defense, goaltending — they were totally out-manned and outclassed at every position…

TG: Were you surprised after (Wayne) Gretzky was sold that the team folded?

DP: It hit me like a ton of bricks. I really wanted to believe that the Racers could survive. I was under a dark cloud for the rest of the hockey season after the team folded. It was so frustrating…

TG: How did the support for the minor league Indianapolis Checkers and Indianapolis Ice in the 1980s and 1990s compare to the Racers in the 1970s?

DP: The city is not nearly as excited now for hockey as it was for the Racers. There were quite a few old Racers fans at games during the Checkers era (the early 1980s), but less and less as the team went on and turned into the Ice. But you could tell the fans' hearts weren't in it, everyone knew it was minor league. And the Fairgrounds Arena doesn't have nearly the atmosphere as the old Market Square Arena. The Racers were the height of hockey in Indy, for sure.

TG: Dave, are you still a SuperFan?

DP: (chuckling) I still yell more than anyone else at any game!

FAN REMEMBRANCE: BRUCE BOGGESS

I was always fascinated by hockey — played by the mysterious Canadians — and what little we ever saw was mostly in the Olympics. My family moved to Indianapolis in 1972 and NBC started to show an NHL game of the week (on TV). Then along came the Racers in 1974, and I remember being awestruck that I would actually have a professional hockey team to watch in person.

Early on, I was excited that I would get to see a lot of great players I had only read about: Gordie Howe, Bobby Hull, Jacques Plante, Frank Mahovlich, and the Racers' own Dave Keon.

I remember Bobby Hull and Gordie Howe were always so nice to fans in Indianapolis. The one time I held a program over the glass for Gordie Howe, he came right over to sign it, and kind of growled "lower" to me. I think I almost separated my arm to get that program low enough for him so I didn't piss him off.

I never saw a Racers player who wouldn't talk to fans for a few minutes, and very early on I became a fan of Ken Block. My friends would go skate at the ice dome at Keystone at the Crossing and he would be there a lot of times watching his little boys skate. When I went to the second Jacques Demers hockey camp he was an instructor and always talked to me and gave a few words of encouragement. To this day anytime I have a number put on a jersey it's always Ken Block's Racers number "24."

Some of my game memories include a game against Cleveland that ended up in a bench-clearing brawl, leaving nothing but gloves and sticks all over the ice — not unusual for the WHA. There was a home game against Cincinnati — just two nights earlier in Cincinnati the game had also turned into a slugfest. The following home game was a sellout, and amazingly no fights broke out! My buddy and me even bought lower-level seats to get a good view of the impending donnybrook (that never occurred).

I also remember games against the amazingly quick Czech and Russian teams, and an opening night crowd (in 1978) giving new owner Nelson Skalbania a standing ovation for "saving" the Racers. I also remember buying the cheapest seats available and then moving around the almost empty arena and sitting wherever I wanted.

There came a point in my ice skating (mostly on a pond in front of a church right beside Crestview Elementary) where I wanted to try real games. The Racers Booster Club had a pick-up game every Sunday, where you pitched in $5 and had a two-hour scrimmage. There were various skill levels and the emphasis was on fun and the enjoyment of playing. I played every Sunday all year around for about four years.

Then I was ready for the (Coach) Jacques Demers' hockey camps. They were an eye opener because I finally learned the drills and workouts that are used on real teams. And it worked — when I would come off the ice at later pick-up games I would almost immediately recover and be ready to go right back out on the ice. I kept those lessons with me playing high school hockey for Lawrence North High School.

I remember one time Coach Demers was a little annoyed at us "big kids" during a checking drill for not hitting very hard. I was next in line and he threw a puck in the corner and told me to go. All I saw was a vision of his blue-clad elbow coming at my head as he rattled me off the boards. So at least I can say that I got slammed by a Stanley Cup winning coach!

I remember all the players as being extremely helpful and supportive. The trainer, Eddie Swiss, was the "hard-ass," and at one point came out and ran us boards-to-boards until I know I was as exhausted as I had ever been.

The band Kiss was playing at Market Square Arena one night I was there training (in the hockey camp). I was leaving the locker room area and was looking through the glass wall separating the outer lobby — and being more than a little freaked out having to walk through all those face-painted older teenagers. And what was that funny smelling smoke?

I ended up working at the Carmel Ice Skadium (yes, "skadium") because most of the other employees played hockey for Carmel High School, and they needed a few other people to cover their game nights. This was my senior year at Lawrence North, playing hockey, and driving the family's Z-28. Looking back, life wasn't all that bad, except for disco music.

The Racers practiced mostly in the mornings and even though I got out of school early that year, they were usually gone when I got there. A couple of times they practiced on Sundays before I had my usual Booster Club pick-up game and the players would be leaving when we were on the ice. Some of them would hang around and watch; it was quite a kick to get encouragement from those guys.

I remember one Saturday the Racers were going to have an early practice open to the public and I was working. Into the shop comes Pat Stapleton looking to get his skates sharpened. I don't think I was ever as careful or spent as much time on any skates than I did on his, even my own. I handed them to him and he said, "Let's take a look," and turned them upside down and placed a penny on the blades to check the sharpening job. I got a "Not bad," and a big smile from him. I don't even remember if I charged him the buck or not.

I remember when Wayne Gretzky was signed. He was supposed to be this wonder boy, even though he was just two months older than I was. I saw all the home exhibition games and the first three regular season 1978-79 home games with Gretzky, but I'll be damned if I can remember anything about him on the ice. I do remember seeing him around the Carmel area at the Steak 'N Shake restaurant. I'm pretty sure he had one of those Trans-Ams with the big decal on the hood. I never really considered that all the other players were older and were off on their own, and he only knew a few people.

I remember during the 1976-77 season there were rumblings about financial problems with the Racers. Even with all the franchise movement that went on in the WHA, I just assumed that the team was going to be around for a long time. Nelson Skalbania saved the team for 1977-78, and I kind of thought there would always be someone who would come along and want to own the franchise.

The next year when four WHA teams were absorbed into the NHL, I remember thinking how the Racers could have been one of those teams. Looking at NHL teams now in places like Columbus, Raleigh and Nashville I think it could be feasible today.

FAN REMEMBRANCE: RANDY GREB

I was only 9 years old when Indianapolis was granted an expansion WHA franchise, and I can thank my older sister for introducing me to the team and the game of hockey. It was in December 1975 and she told me we were going to a Racers game — but to be honest I thought she said a Pacers (basketball) game.

I was able to see about 20 games while the team was here but to be sure I listened to every other game on the radio without fail. The team was on WART-FM (and WIBC-AM) at the time and Bob Lamey fueled my imagination as I listened to my beloved team. I was also at Game 7 of the 1976 playoff series with New England, and even though we lost that game 6-0 the crowd never stopped cheering. It was magical.

The city and fans finally got a special gift in April 1977 when we met the hated Cincinnati Stingers in the first round of the playoffs. Cincy finished ahead of us in the standings and received the home ice advantage. They were favored against the Racers, and Game 1 on April 9, 1977 in Cincinnati will go down in Racers history. I watched the whole game in Indianapolis on TV's Channel 4 — the Stingers took a 3-2 lead with a Claude Larose goal with only 2:39 left and I thought that was the killer. But one of my favorite Racers, Reggie Thomas, tied the game with 1:04 left. I was exhausted with joy, but so much more was yet to come.

The game went into sudden death overtime, and two additional 20-minute periods came and went without a goal — but had many, many close calls. Thank God that game was not on a school night — the third overtime period began and it was well past one in the morning!

Bob Lamey's voice was all but gone in the third OT, but when I heard him shout, "Peacosh shoots....SCORE!" I screamed and my Dad came into the room and told me to settle down and go to bed. But I listened to the post game on the radio and couldn't sleep all night. The Racers went on to sweep the favored Stingers, closing them out 3-1 one week later in front of a capacity Indy crowd.

We went on to face the Nordiques, which won 11 more games than the Racers that year, and with Real Cloutier and Serge Bernier they would be the toughest test ever for the young Racers. We fell down two games to none and a Game 3 overtime loss (6-5) took the steam out of the team. I went to Game 4 at MSA and a huge crowd fueled the team to a 2-0 shutout win against the eventual AVCO Cup champions. Sadly it was one of the last special moments we would have with the Racers. The team was closed out 8-3 in Québec City in Game 5 and a storybook season was over.

Letting Jacques Demers go to Cincinnati and the loss of other gritty players spelled disaster for the 1977-1978 season, which ended with a last place finish. I really despised the management moves that crippled our team and I knew these were the first steps that would end the beloved franchise. The one memorable item from that season was the home-and-home brawls that took place between the Racers and the Birmingham Bulls. There were hundreds of penalty minutes in both games that led to quite a few suspensions. I was also able to go to a few games against the Czech team and the Russian teams in 1978.

One has to wonder that if we had better management in 1977 and 1978 if we would have been one of those teams invited to join the NHL in 1979 — having Gretzky and Messier could have been a ticket to a different history for hockey in Indianapolis.

The city enjoyed some excitement after the Racers, with the minor-league Checkers and Ice winning championships — but hockey in Indianapolis never recovered from the mismanagement of the Racers and the breaking of thousands of hearts.

Pat Stapleton: "The General" of the defense from 1975-1977, and Head Coach for late 1978.

RACERS ALL-STARS (left to right): **Pat Stapleton, Hugh Harris, Jacques Demers** (Coach), **Michel Parizeau** and **Blair MacDonald** represented the Indianapolis Racers at the 1977 WHA All-Star game in Hartford on January 18, 1977. It was the largest All-Star contingent for Indianapolis in the history of the franchise.

TOP: The Racers' **Dick Proceviat** handles the puck at home against **Edmonton**, 1977. **The Oilers** are the only WHA team that survived without interruption all the way from the rebel league's initial 1972 season, through the 1979 merger with the NHL, through today. They're also the only former WHA team to win the NHL's Stanley Cup.

BOTTOM: A peek at the Racers bench in Market Square Arena, during the initial 1974-1975 season.

TOP LEFT:
Classic WIBC radio voice and Indy sports announcing legend **"Hockey Bob" Lamey**.

BOTTOM LEFT:
Talented forward **Blair "BJ" MacDonald**, who would go on to the Edmonton Oilers as one of **Wayne Gretzky**'s linemates.

RIGHT:
Hall of Famer **Dave Keon** found a temporary playing home in Indianapolis in 1976.

TOP LEFT:
All-Star defenseman **Darryl Maggs** (note the NHL Washington Capitals player in the background).

BOTTOM LEFT:
Goalie **Jim Park** stops "Mr. Hockey," **Gordie Howe**. *(courtesy Jim Park)*

RIGHT: A triumphant fan favorite, forward **Brian McDonald**.

Previously unpublished team promo photos:

UPPER LEFT: Ted Scharf vs. New England.
UPPER RIGHT: Reg Thomas vs. Denver.
LOWER LEFT: Dick Proceviat vs. San Diego.
LOWER RIGHT: Pat Stapleton vs. Baltimore. Notice **Billy Goldthorpe** (at far right with the afro hair) on the bench behind Stapleton — Goldthorpe was the inspiration for the outlandish character "Ogie Ogilthorpe" in the classic 1977 hockey film comedy "Slapshot."

1977 PLAYOFFS: INDIANAPOLIS 4, CINCINNATI 0

Goalie **Paul Hoganson** (left) keeps an eagle eye on the puck while defenseman **Bryon Baltimore** and friends (right) patrol the crease during the 1977 WHA playoff sweep of the favored **Cincinnati Stingers**.

Hoganson was brilliant in the playoff series, inspired to prove his worth to his former Stinger teammates. The playoff sweep would be the apex for the Racers franchise and its fans.

(bottom photo by Greg Griffo, courtesy The Indianapolis Star)

TOP:
Racers Booster **Don Wahle** is delighted, and **Gene Peacosh** looks a bit surprised, that a trophy exists to celebrate the Racers' 1976-1977 regular season series win over rival Cincinnati.

BOTTOM:
Don Wahle (far left) with **Ken Block** (Team MVP, sitting), Coach **Jacques Demers**, and **Michel Dion** (Team Rookie of the Year, far right) at the end of the 1975-1976 championship season. Dion would also earn the WHA Best Goaltender award for the season.

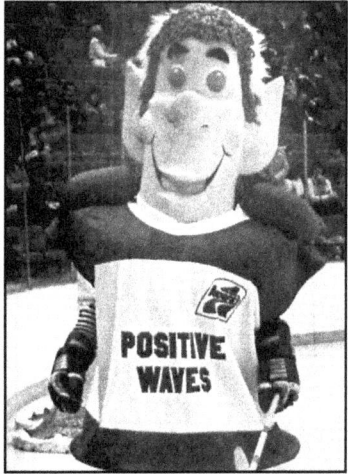

UPPER LEFT: Author **Timothy Gassen** (left), then age 16, gives an award to TV Channel 6 Sports Anchor and Racers supporter **Craig Roberts** in 1977 as a North Central High School classmate looks on.

UPPER RIGHT: Elf-like mascot **"Moriarty"** attempts to stay on his skates.

BOTTOM: Racers favorites (left to right) **Michel Dion**, **Kim Clackson**, **Brian McDonald**, **Hugh Harris** and **Ted Scharf** seem to enjoy the antics of the **SuperFans** high in the rafters of Market Square Arena, circa 1976.

(Author photo: North Central Northern Lights)

RACERS BOSSES:
(Clockwise, from upper right): Coach **Jacques Demers**, Coach **Gerry Moore**, final team owner **Nelson Skalbania**, player-coach **Bill Goldsworthy**, Coach **Ron Ingram**. Former defenseman **Pat Stapleton** would be the team's last Head Coach, starting the 1978-1979 season.

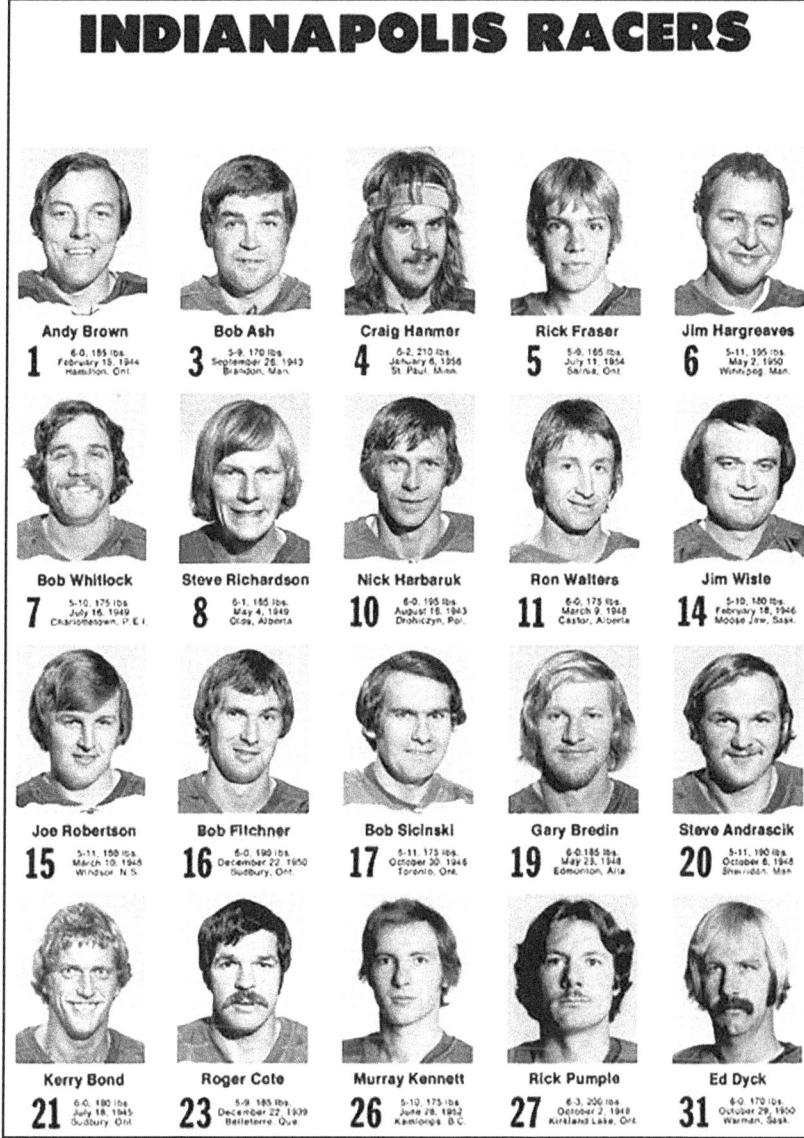

1974-1975 opening night roster:

Losing and losing big, the Racers made drastic lineup alterations by the middle of their first season — and only three players from this opening night roster would make it to the second season (**Nick Harbaruk**, **Andy Brown** & **Bob Sicinski**).

The WHA created hundreds of new jobs in major league hockey, but the glut of teams made the job of building a winner even more difficult.

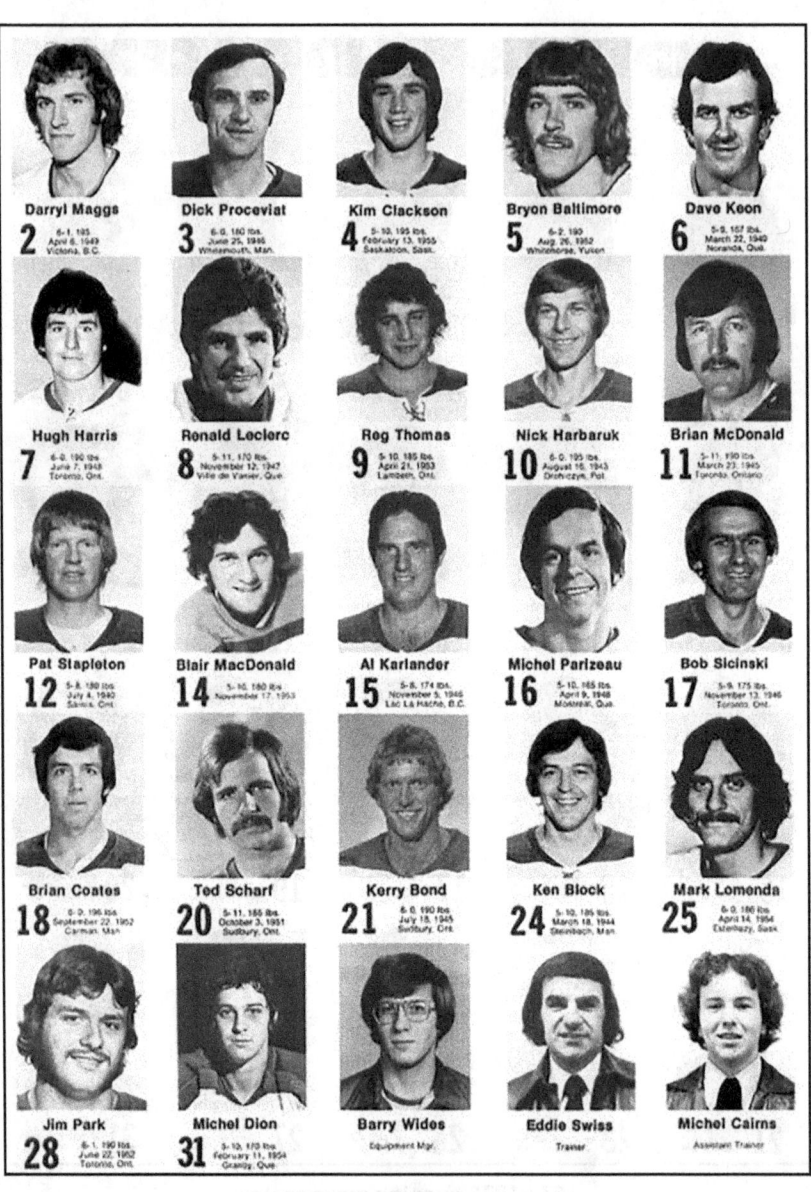

1975-1976 playoff roster:

The talent level of the second-year Racers rose dramatically by mid-season, and the competitive team caught fire in Indy. Notice Hall of Famer **Dave Keon** in the upper right — he joined the Racers late in the season to help push them into their first playoff berth. Amazingly, the Racers would win the WHA's Eastern Division and equal the New England Whalers before falling in Game Seven of their first playoff series.

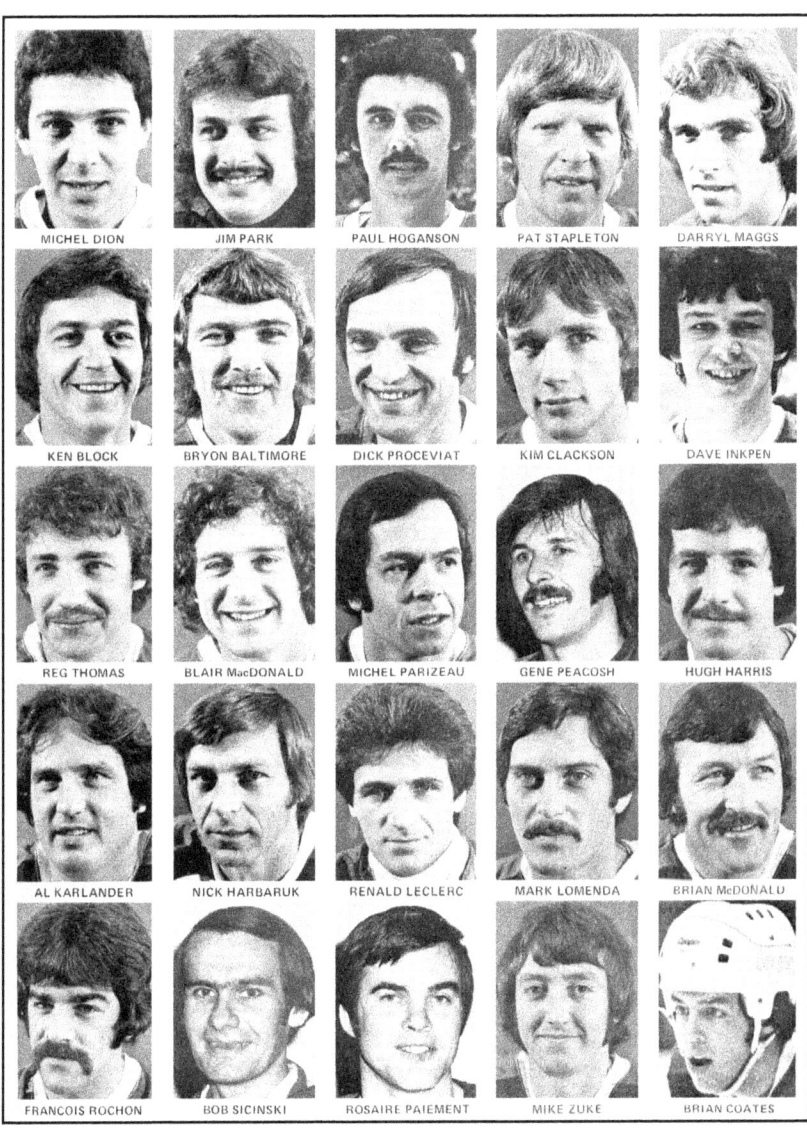

1976-1977 playoff roster:

The goaltending trio of **Michel Dion**, **Jim Park** and **Paul Hoganson** proved to be among the finest in all of hockey in the regular season of 1977, and that year's playoff performance of the entire team was the pinnacle for the franchise.

Though firing on all cylinders in the 4-0 playoff sweep of dreaded rivals Cincinnati, the Racers couldn't match the firepower of eventual WHA champs Québec in the semi-final round.

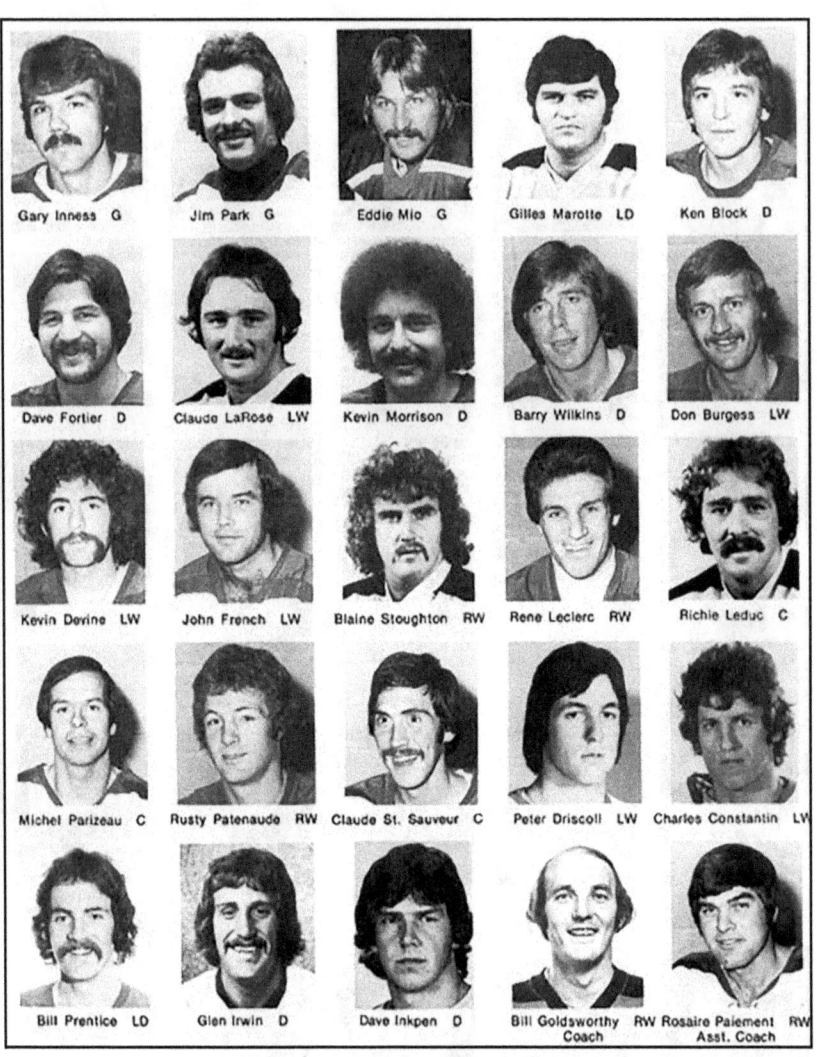

1977-1978 late-season roster:

With the competitive mainstays of the team suddenly gone, the Racers line-up returned to the revolving door of the first season, with disastrous results.

Notice player-coach **Bill Goldsworthy** (lower right); ineffective Head Coach **Ron Ingram** had been curtly dismissed by team owner **Nelson Skalbania** 51 games into the season. Winger **Rosaire Paiement** also moved to the bench as an Assistant Coach after suffering a serious injury.

The moves didn't change the Racers' position at the bottom of the standings.

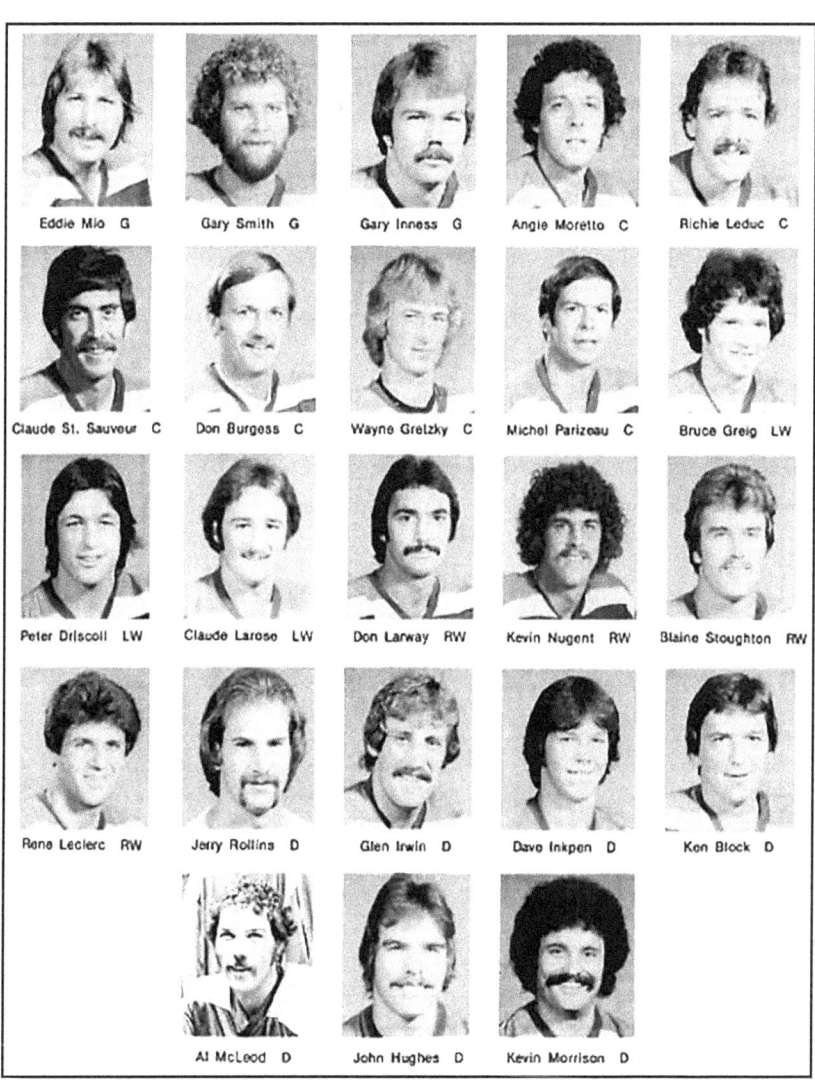

1978-1979 early-season roster:

The final Racers roster saw rookie **Wayne Gretzky** (middle second row) surrounded by another new team lineup.

Franchise favorites **Ken Block**, **Rene LeClerc** and **Michel Parizeau** were the only remaining pieces of the competitive and popular teams of 1975-1977. Only a few weeks into the season, Gretzky would pack his bags for Edmonton, glory, Stanley Cups, and the Hockey Hall of Fame.

Major league hockey would pack its bags and leave Indianapolis in December of 1978.

A Racers promo photo given to members of the "Great Gretzky" fan club in 1978.

99 GRETZKY, Wayne

CENTER

HGT./WGT.: 5'11"/165
BORN: January 26, 1961
Brantford, Ontario

CAREER RECORD

Year	Team	League	GP	G	A	PTS	PIM
1977-78	Sault Ste. Marie	OHL	64	70	112	182	14

THE YOUNG GREAT ONE:

LEFT: The 17-year-old's entry in the Racers' 1978-1979 Media Guide.

He'd fill in the records section nicely as his career went along.

INDIANAPOLIS RACERS FRANCHISE STATISTICS

The all-time Racers player roster is courtesy of the kind permission of Ralph Slate and his indispensable **www.hockeydb.com** Web site. Statistics that follow after the all-time roster are courtesy of the kind permission of Scott Adam Surgent and his essential book, "The Complete Historical and Statistical Reference to the World Hockey Association" (available through **www.xalerpress.com**). The author has edited, added, and organized some additional data and details below.

HOME ICE
Market Square Arena, downtown Indianapolis, Indiana (capacity 16,040)
Team Colors: red, white & blue
First game: October 17, 1974
Last game: December 12, 1978

RACERS SEASON RESULTS

Season	GP	W	L	T	Pts	Win %	GF	GA	PIM	Playoffs
1974-75	78	18	57	3	39	0.250	216	338	970	none
1975-76	80	35	39	6	76*	0.475	245	247	1301	lost in round 1
1976-77	81	36	37	8	80	0.494	276	305	880	lost in round 2
1977-78	80	24	51	5	53	0.331	267	353	1189	none
1978-79	25	5	18	2	12	0.240	78	130	557	none

*1976 World Hockey Association Eastern Division regular season champions

PLAYOFF RESULTS

Year	GP	W	L
1976	7	3	4
1977	8	5	4

INTERNATIONAL PLAY
December 22, 1976: Racers 3, Czechoslovakia 2
January 1, 1977: Soviets 5, Racers 2
Dec 9, 1977: Czechoslovakia 5, Racers 3
December 18, 1977: Soviets 4, Racers 3
January 1, 1978: Soviets 4, Racers 2
January 10, 1978: Soviets 8, Racers 3
March 17, 1978: Racers 6, Sweden 3
March 22, 1978: Finland 4, Racers 3

EXHIBITION GAMES AGAINST THE NHL
October 4, 1974: Detroit Red Wings 3, Racers 3 (at Ft. Wayne, IN)
September 26, 1976: Washington Capitals 2, Racers 1 September 30, 1976: Pittsburgh Penguins 6, Racers 4
October 6, 1978: Racers 4, St. Louis Blues 1

HEAD COACHES

Coach	Years	Games	W-L-T
Gerry Moore	74-75	83	19-61-3
Jacques Demers	75-77	156	78-80-14*
Ron Ingram	77-78	51	16-31-4
Bill Goldsworthy	77-78	29	8-20-1
Pat Stapleton	78-79	25	5-18-2

* includes an 8-8 record in playoffs

INDIANAPOLIS RACERS FRANCHISE STATISTICS

GENERAL MANAGERS
James Browitt (1974-1976)
Brian Conacher (1976-1977)
Ron Ingram (1977-1978)
Pat Stapleton (1978-1979)

FRANCHISE RECORDS
Single Season:
Goals	36	Claude St. Sauveur (1977-78)
Assists	55	Darryl Maggs (1976-77)
Points	78	Claude St. Sauveur (1977-78)
PIM	351	Kim Clackson (1975-76)
Wins	17	Michel Dion (1976-77)
SOs	2	Andy Brown (1974-75); Jim Park (1976 playoffs)
GAA	2.74	Michel Dion (1975-76)

All-Time:
Games	267	Ken Block (1974-78)
Goals	63	Reg Thomas (1975-78)
Assists	88	Michel Parizeau (1976-78)
Points	136	Michel Parizeau (1976-78)
PIM	519	Kim Clackson (1975-77)
Wins	31	Michel Dion (1975-77)
SOs	3	Andy Brown (1974-76); Jim Park (1975-1977, including playoffs)
GAA	3.08	Michel Dion (1975-77)

RACERS ALL-STARS & AWARD WINNERS
Year-End All-Star Team: Pat Stapleton, Second Team, 1975-76; Darryl Maggs, First Team, 1976-77

Mid-Season All-Star Game: Andy Brown, 1975; Pat Stapleton, 1976 & 1977; Michel Parizeau, Hugh Harris and Blair MacDonald, 1977; Rusty Patenaude, 1978. Coach Jacques Demers coached the Eastern All-Stars in the 1977 game.

1976 Ben Hatskin Award (for best goaltender):
Michel Dion, 2.74 Goals Against Average

RADIO & TELEVISION COVERAGE
1974-77: Radio WIBC 1070 AM, "Hockey" Bob Lamey;
TV WTTV Channel 4, Lee Hamilton
1977-78; Radio WIBC 1070 AM & WART 100.9 FM, Mike Fornes & Chet Coppock
1978-79: Radio WIBC 1070 AM, Mike Fornes & Al Karlander

RACERS HOME GAME ATTENDANCE
Season	Games	Total Attendance	Average per game	Playoff average
1974-75	39	309,005	7,923	none
1975-76	40	351,127	8,778	12,087
1976-77	40	371,787	9,295*	12,717
1977-78	41	301,891	7,363	none
1978-79	13	82,727	6,364	none

*led league in attendance for season

RACERS ALL-TIME PLAYER ROSTER

Player	GP	G	A	Pts	PIM	Seasons	Yrs.
Ray Adduono	8	1	2	3	0	1977-78	1
Steve Andrascik	20	2	4	6	16	1974-75	1
Bob Ash	64	1	14	15	19	1974-75	1
Bryon Baltimore	116	3	33	36	118	1975-79	4
Bill Blackwood	3	0	0	0	0	1977-78	1
Ken Block	267	7	80	87	115	1974-79	5
Kerry Bond	86	24	15	39	32	1974-76	2
Gary Bredin	10	3	2	5	8	1974-75	1
Andy Brown (G)	86	0	4	4	92	1974-77	3
Ron Buchanan	55	20	22	42	20	1974-76	2
Randy Burchell (G)	5	0	1	1	0	1976-77	1
Don Burgess	82	12	13	25	2	1977-79	2
Bryan Campbell	8	1	4	5	6	1976-77	1
Kim Clackson	148	4	20	24	519	1975-77	2
Brian Coates	75	12	21	33	28	1975-77	2
Charles Constantin	6	2	1	3	0	1977-78	1
Roger Cote	36	0	6	6	24	1974-75	1
Glen Critch	3	0	0	0	0	1975-76	1
Ken Desjardine	46	0	8	8	68	1974-75	1
Kevin Devine	76	19	23	42	141	1977-78	1
Michel Dion (G)	74	0	0	0	2	1974-77	3
Dave Dornseif	3	0	1	1	0	1977-78	1
Peter Driscoll	64	28	22	50	147	1977-79	2
Michel Dubois	34	2	2	4	104	1975-76	1
Ed Dyck (G)	32	0	0	0	6	1974-75	1
Bob Fitchner	130	26	35	61	208	1974-76	2
Dave Fortier	54	1	15	16	86	1977-78	1
Rick Fraser	4	0	0	0	2	1974-75	1
John French	74	9	8	17	6	1977-78	1
Wes George	9	4	2	6	23	1978-79	1
Bill Goldsworthy	32	8	10	18	10	1977-78	1
Bruce Greig	21	3	7	10	64	1978-79	1
Wayne Gretzky	8	3	3	6	0	1978-79	1
Craig Hamner	27	1	0	1	15	1974-75	1
Nick Harbaruk	181	45	44	89	80	1974-77	3
Joe Hardy	32	2	17	19	36	1974-75	1
Jim Hargreaves	37	2	5	7	30	1974-75	1
Hugh Harris	106	34	70	104	50	1975-78	3
Murray Heatley	63	17	13	30	32	1974-76	2
Paul Hoganson (G)	11	0	0	0	2	1976-77	1
Leif Holmquist (G)	19	0	0	0	4	1975-76	1
Ralph Hopiavouri	28	2	8	10	21	1974-75	1
Bill Horton	59	2	9	11	30	1974-75	1
John Hughes	22	3	4	7	48	1978-79	1
Dave Inkpen	81	6	29	35	66	1976-79	3
Gary Inness (G)	62	0	0	0	51	1977-79	2
Glen Irwin	44	0	1	1	196	1977-79	2

RACERS ALL-TIME PLAYER ROSTER

Player	GP	G	A	Pts	PIM	Seasons	Yrs.
Jim Johnson	42	7	15	22	12	1974-75	1
Bob Jones	2	0	0	0	0	1975-76	1
Gordon Kannegiesser	4	1	4	5	4	1974-75	1
Al Karlander	144	33	56	89	59	1975-77	2
Murray Kennett	28	1	3	4	8	1974-75	1
Dave Keon	12	3	7	10	2	1975-76	1
Claude Larose	41	19	24	43	12	1977-79	2
Don Larway	25	8	10	18	39	1978-79	1
Rene LeClerc	190	60	73	133	138	1975-79	4
Rich Leduc	41	15	24	39	52	1977-79	2
Gerry Leroux	10	0	3	3	2	1978-79	1
Jacques Locas	11	0	1	1	2	1974-75	1
Mark Lomenda	58	9	12	21	14	1975-77	2
Blair MacDonald	137	53	41	94	42	1975-77	2
Gary MacGregor	33	8	9	17	4	1976-79	2
Dean Magee	5	0	1	1	10	1978-79	1
Darryl Maggs	168	27	86	113	184	1975-78	3
Gilles Marotte	44	2	13	15	18	1977-78	1
Larry Mavety	10	2	2	4	8	1976-77	1
Brian McDonald	159	45	45	90	125	1974-77	3
Peter McDuffe (G)	12	0	0	0	0	1977-78	1
Brian McKenzie	9	1	0	1	6	1974-75	1
Al McLeod	25	0	11	11	22	1978-79	1
Mark Messier	5	0	0	0	0	1978-79	1
Eddie Mio (G)	22	0	0	0	2	1977-79	2
Angie Moretto	18	3	1	4	2	1978-79	1
Kevin Morrison	80	17	42	59	49	1977-79	2
Dave Morrow	10	2	10	12	29	1978-79	1
Kevin Nugent	25	2	8	10	20	1978-79	1
Rosaire Paiement	128	24	49	73	172	1976-78	2
Michel Parizeau	190	48	88	136	110	1975-79	4
Jim Park (G)	54	0	2	2	14	1975-78	3
Ed Patenaude	76	23	19	42	71	1977-78	1
Gene Peacosh	64	22	26	48	21	1976-77	1
Lynn Powis	14	4	6	10	2	1977-78	1
Bill Prentice	59	5	3	8	120	1975-78	2
Dick Proceviat	180	10	53	63	115	1974-77	3
Rich Pumple	34	4	8	12	29	1974-75	1
Brad Rhiness	12	3	3	6	2	1977-78	1
Steve Richardson	19	1	4	5	16	1974-75	1
Joe Robertson	18	4	4	8	23	1974-75	1
Frank Rochon	76	21	10	31	39	1975-77	2
Jerry Rollins	7	0	1	1	7	1978-79	1
Bob Roselle	1	0	0	0	0	1975-76	1
Larry Sacharuk	15	2	9	11	25	1978-79	1
Ted Scharf	74	7	13	20	56	1975-76	1
Bobby Sheehan	29	8	7	15	6	1977-78	1

RACERS ALL-TIME PLAYER ROSTER

Player	GP	G	A	Pts	PIM	Seasons	Yrs.
John Sheridan	69	18	13	31	20	1974-76	2
Bob Sicinski	207	40	92	132	30	1974-77	3
Dale Smedsmo	6	0	3	3	7	1977-78	1
Gary Smith (G)	11	0	0	0	8	1978-79	1
Ross Smith	15	1	6	7	19	1974-75	1
Frank Spring	13	2	4	6	2	1977-78	1
Claude St. Sauveur	89	40	44	84	36	1977-79	2
Pat Stapleton	161	13	85	98	77	1975-77	2
Blaine Stoughton	72	22	22	44	44	1977-79	2
Reg Thomas	208	63	63	126	101	1975-78	3
Ron Walters	17	2	1	3	9	1974-75	1
Bob Whitlock	103	38	41	79	72	1974-76	2
Barry Wilkins	79	2	21	23	79	1977-78	1
Jim Wiste	82	13	30	43	30	1974-76	2
Bob Woytowich	84	1	15	16	42	1974-76	2
Randy Wyrozub	55	11	14	25	8	1975-76	1
Mike Zuke	15	3	4	7	2	1976-77	1

(G) = Goaltender

RACERS ALL-TIME INTRALEAGUE RECORD

	all-time					home					away				
opponent	w	l	t	gf	ga	w	l	t	gf	ga	w	l	t	gf	ga
Chicago	2	3	1	24	24	2	1	0	11	8	0	2	1	13	16
Cincinnati	17	19	1	121	147	12	6	1	76	60	5	13	0	45	87
Cle/Min	8	12	0	64	75	6	4	0	36	32	2	8	0	28	43
Denver	1	3	0	14	13	0	2	0	6	10	1	1	0	8	3
Edmonton	8	19	1	91	130	6	9	0	48	52	2	10	1	43	78
Houston	10	18	2	85	124	6	8	2	47	64	4	10	0	38	60
Mich/Balt	4	2	0	30	19	1	2	0	13	12	3	0	0	17	7
Minnesota (orig.)	1	9	0	31	46	1	4	0	13	19	0	5	0	18	27
New England	17	18	8	142	157	9	8	3	67	67	8	10	5	75	90
Phoenix	5	12	1	46	78	4	5	0	27	28	1	7	1	19	50
Québec	12	21	1	118	148	9	7	1	68	71	3	14	0	50	77
San Diego	4	10	4	49	67	4	4	1	27	28	0	6	3	22	39
Tor/Bir	17	16	2	114	126	11	6	0	69	56	6	10	2	45	70
Van/Cgy	4	10	2	39	55	3	4	1	22	28	1	6	1	17	27
Winnipeg	8	25	1	95	155	5	13	0	63	86	3	12	1	32	69
Touring teams	0	2	0	6	9	0	2	0	6	9	-	-	-	-	-

1974-1975 INDIANAPOLIS RACERS Game Results
Coach: Gerry Moore 18-57-3   (* away game)

	date		opponent	score		w	l	t	pts	gf	ga
1	Oct 17		Michigan	2-4	L	0	1	0	0	2	4
2	Oct 18	*	Toronto	1-3	L	0	2	0	0	3	7
3	Oct 20	*	Québec	1-4	L	0	3	0	0	4	11
4	Oct 24		Minnesota	2-3	L	0	4	0	0	6	14
5	Oct 26	*	New England	1-6	L	0	5	0	0	7	20
6	Oct 27		Québec	5-3	W	1	5	0	2	12	23
7	Oct 31		New England	1-6	L	1	6	0	2	13	29
8	Nov 3		Edmonton	1-3	L	1	7	0	2	14	32
9	Nov 5		Phoenix	0-3	L	1	8	0	2	14	35
10	Nov 7		San Diego	3-0	W	2	8	0	4	17	35
11	Nov 9	*	Houston	5-4	W-ot	3	8	0	6	22	39
12	Nov 10	*	Michigan	6-1	W	4	8	0	8	28	40
13	Nov 13	*	Québec	3-10	L	4	9	0	8	31	50
14	Nov 15	*	Winnipeg	0-5	L	4	10	0	8	31	55
15	Nov 17	*	Edmonton	1-2	L	4	11	0	8	32	57
16	Nov 19		Houston	0-10	L	4	12	0	8	32	67
17	Nov 20	*	Chicago	4-6	L	4	13	0	8	36	73
18	Nov 21		New England	0-4	L	4	14	0	8	36	77
19	Nov 24		Toronto	2-9	L	4	15	0	8	38	86
20	Nov 26		Winnipeg	0-4	L	4	16	0	8	38	90
21	Nov 28		Québec	5-7	L	4	17	0	8	43	97
22	Nov 29	*	Cleveland	2-4	L	4	18	0	8	45	101
23	Dec 1		Houston	3-7	L	4	19	0	8	48	108
24	Dec 5		Chicago	3-5	L	4	20	0	8	51	113
25	Dec 7	*	New England	3-6	L	4	21	0	8	54	119
26	Dec 8		San Diego	5-3	W	5	21	0	10	59	122
27	Dec 10		Winnipeg	3-5	L	5	22	0	10	62	127
28	Dec 14	*	San Diego	0-2	L	5	23	0	10	62	129
29	Dec 15		Edmonton	1-3	L	5	24	0	10	63	132
30	Dec 17		Vancouver	2-3	L	5	25	0	10	65	135
31	Dec 19		Minnesota	0-6	L	5	26	0	10	65	141
32	Dec 20	*	Minnesota	4-6	L	5	27	0	10	69	147
33	Dec 22		New England	2-1	W	6	27	0	12	71	148
34	Dec 27	*	Vancouver	1-1	T	6	27	1	13	72	149
35	Dec 29	*	Edmonton	4-5	L-ot	6	28	1	13	76	154
36	Jan 1	*	Québec	3-6	L	6	29	1	13	79	160
37	Jan 2	*	Cleveland	1-4	L	6	30	1	13	80	164
38	Jan 4	*	Chicago	4-4	T	6	30	2	14	84	168
39	Jan 5		Phoenix	1-2	L	6	31	2	14	85	170
			First half record:			6	31	2	14	85	170

	date		opponent	score		w	l	t	pts	gf	ga
40	Jan 7		Vancouver	4-2	W	7	31	2	16	89	172
41	Jan 10	*	Edmonton	3-3	T	7	31	3	17	92	175
42	Jan 16		Cleveland	4-2	W	8	31	3	19	96	177
43	Jan 19	*	Vancouver	1-5	L	8	32	3	19	97	182
44	Jan 22	*	Winnipeg	3-1	W	9	32	3	21	100	183
45	Jan 23		Chicago	4-2	W	10	32	3	23	104	185
46	Jan 26	*	Phoenix	0-6	L	10	33	3	23	104	191
47	Jan 28		Phoenix	1-3	L	10	34	3	23	105	194
48	Jan 30		Toronto	2-3	L	10	35	3	23	107	197
49	Feb 1		Québec	1-2	L	10	36	3	23	108	199
50	Feb 4		Houston	3-4	L- ot	10	37	3	23	111	203
51	Feb 9	*	Toronto	5-7	L	10	38	3	23	116	210
52	Feb 10		Chicago	4-1	W	11	38	3	25	120	211

134

	date		opponent	score		w	l	t	pts	gf	ga
53	Feb 14	*	New England	3-4	L- ot	11	39	3	25	123	215
54	Feb 17	*	Chicago	5-6	L	11	40	3	25	128	221
55	Feb 18		Vancouver	2-9	L	11	41	3	25	130	230
56	Feb 21		Minnesota	5-2	W	12	41	3	27	135	232
57	Feb 23		Cleveland	6-0	W	13	41	3	29	141	232
58	Feb 25	*	Baltimore	6-4	W	14	41	3	31	147	236
59	Feb 26	*	Minnesota	3-4	L- ot	14	42	3	31	150	240
60	Mar 1	*	Phoenix	2-12	L	14	43	3	31	152	252
61	Mar 2	*	Houston	3-4	L- ot	14	44	3	31	155	256
62	Mar 5	*	Baltimore	5-2	W	15	44	3	33	160	258
63	Mar 7		Baltimore	4-5	L- ot	15	45	3	33	164	263
64	Mar 8		Cleveland	5-6	L	15	46	3	33	169	269
65	Mar 13		Toronto	5-4	W	16	46	3	35	174	273
66	Mar 15		Baltimore	7-3	W	17	46	3	37	181	276
67	Mar 19	*	Houston	5-6	L	17	47	3	37	186	282
68	Mar 20		Edmonton	3-1	W	18	47	3	39	189	283
69	Mar 22	*	San Diego	3-6	L	18	48	3	39	192	289
70	Mar 23	*	Phoenix	3-5	L	18	49	3	39	195	294
71	Mar 25		Winnipeg	3-4	L- ot	18	50	3	39	198	298
72	Mar 27		San Diego	2-5	L	18	51	3	39	200	303
73	Mar 29	*	Cleveland	5-7	L	18	52	3	39	205	310
74	Mar 30	*	Minnesota	3-5	L	18	53	3	39	208	315
75	Mar 31	*	Winnipeg	1-4	L	18	54	3	39	209	319
76	Apr 1	*	Toronto	1-7	L	18	55	3	39	210	326
77	Apr 5	*	San Diego	3-8	L	18	56	3	39	213	334
78	Apr 6	*	Vancouver	3-4	L	18	57	3	39	216	338
			Second half record:			12	26	1	25	131	168

RECORD VS. OPPONENTS

opponent	season					home					away				
	w	l	t	gf	ga	w	l	t	gf	ga	w	l	t	gf	ga
Chicago	2	3	1	24	24	2	1	0	11	8	0	2	1	13	16
Cleveland	2	4	0	23	23	2	1	0	16	8	0	3	0	8	15
Edmonton	1	4	1	13	17	1	2	0	5	7	0	2	1	8	10
Houston	1	5	0	19	35	0	3	0	6	21	1	2	0	13	14
Mich./Balt.	4	2	0	30	19	1	2	0	13	12	3	0	0	17	7
Minnesota	1	5	0	17	26	1	2	0	7	11	0	3	0	10	15
New England	1	5	0	10	27	1	2	0	3	11	0	3	0	7	16
Phoenix	0	6	0	7	31	0	3	0	2	8	0	3	0	5	23
Québec	1	5	0	18	32	1	2	0	11	12	0	3	0	7	20
San Diego	2	4	0	16	24	2	1	0	10	8	0	3	0	6	16
Toronto	1	5	0	16	33	1	2	0	9	16	0	3	0	7	17
Vancouver	1	4	1	13	24	1	2	0	8	14	0	2	1	5	10
Winnipeg	1	5	0	10	23	0	3	0	6	13	1	2	0	4	10
TOTAL	18	57	3	216	338	13	26	0	106	149	5	31	3	110	189

RECORD BY MONTH

month	season					home					away				
	w	l	t	gf	ga	w	l	t	gf	ga	w	l	t	gf	ga
October	1	6	0	13	29	1	3	0	10	16	0	3	0	3	13
November	3	12	0	32	72	1	7	0	11	40	2	5	0	21	32
December	2	10	1	31	53	2	6	0	19	33	0	4	1	12	20
January	4	7	2	31	43	3	3	0	16	14	1	4	2	15	29
February	4	7	0	43	43	3	3	0	21	18	1	4	0	22	25
March	4	12	0	59	79	3	4	0	29	28	1	8	0	30	51
April	0	3	0	7	19	-	-	-	-	-	0	3	0	7	19
TOTAL	18	57	3	216	338	13	26	0	106	149	5	31	3	110	189

1975-1976 INDIANAPOLIS RACERS Game Results
Coaches: Gerry Moore 1-4-0; Jacques Demers 34-35-6   (* away game)

	date		opponent	score		w	l	t	pts	gf	ga
1	Oct 10	*	Denver	7-1	W	1	0	0	2	7	1
2	Oct 12	*	Edmonton	5-6	L	1	1	0	2	12	7
3	Oct 14	*	Calgary	3-5	L	1	2	0	2	15	12
4	Oct 16	*	San Diego	0-3	L	1	3	0	2	15	15
5	Oct 18		Denver	4-6	L	1	4	0	2	19	21
6	Oct 21		Minnesota	1-2	L	1	5	0	2	20	23
7	Oct 23		Houston	4-0	W	2	5	0	4	24	23
8	Oct 26		Edmonton	4-3	W	3	5	0	6	28	26
9	Oct 30		Calgary	5-7	L	3	6	0	6	33	33
10	Nov 1		Québec	2-5	L	3	7	0	6	35	38
11	Nov 4		Toronto	4-3	W	4	7	0	8	39	41
12	Nov 8	*	Québec	2-3	L	4	8	0	8	41	44
13	Nov 15	*	Minnesota	7-9	L	4	9	0	8	48	53
14	Nov 16	*	Winnipeg	1-2	L	4	10	0	8	49	55
15	Nov 17	*	Toronto	6-2	W	5	10	0	10	55	57
16.	Nov 19		New England	3-1	W	6	10	0	12	58	58
17	Nov 25	*	Houston	1-4	L	6	11	0	12	59	62
18	Nov 27		Winnipeg	3-1	W	7	11	0	14	62	63
19	Nov 28	*	Cleveland	3-1	W	8	11	0	16	65	64
20	Nov 29	*	New England	3-2	W	9	11	0	18	68	66
21	Nov 30		Denver	2-4	L	9	12	0	18	70	70
22	Dec 4		Cincinnati	7-1	W	10	12	0	20	77	71
23	Dec 6		Cleveland	3-2	W	11	12	0	22	80	73
24	Dec 10	*	Phoenix	2-1	W	12	12	0	24	82	74
25	Dec 11	*	San Diego	3-3	T	12	12	1	25	85	77
26	Dec 12	*	Houston	2-4	L	12	13	1	25	87	81
27	Dec 14		New England	2-2	T	12	13	2	26	89	83
28	Dec 16		Edmonton	1-3	L	12	14	2	26	90	86
29	Dec 18	*	Phoenix	1-7	L	12	15	2	26	91	93
30	Dec 19		Cleveland	5-4	W-ot	13	15	2	28	96	97
31	Dec 20	*	Cleveland	3-5	L	13	16	2	28	99	102
32	Dec 27		Cincinnati	2-1	W	14	16	2	30	101	103
33	Dec 28	*	Cincinnati	1-4	L	14	17	2	30	102	107
34	Dec 30	*	Denver	1-2	L-ot	14	18	2	30	103	109
35	Jan 2		San Diego	0-2	L	14	19	2	30	103	111
36	Jan 3	*	Minnesota	1-3	L	14	20	2	30	104	114
37	Jan 4		New England	3-2	W	15	20	2	32	107	116
38	Jan 6	*	Edmonton	0-3	L	15	21	2	32	107	119
39	Jan 7	*	Calgary	1-3	L	15	22	2	32	108	122
40	Jan 9	*	Winnipeg	2-1	W-ot	16	22	2	34	110	123
			First half record:			16	22	2	34	110	123

	date		opponent	score		w	l	t	pts	gf	ga
41	Jan 11	*	Cleveland	3-4	L	16	23	2	34	113	127
42	Jan 15		Cleveland	1-3	L	16	24	2	34	114	130
43	Jan 17		Cincinnati	0-4	L	16	25	2	34	114	134
44	Jan 21	*	Québec	2-3	L	16	26	2	34	116	137
45	Jan 23		Cincinnati	4-3	W	17	26	2	36	120	140
46	Jan 25		Cleveland	4-2	W	18	26	2	38	124	142
47	Jan 28	*	New England	4-6	L	18	27	2	38	128	148
48	Jan 29		Minnesota	5-6	L	18	28	2	38	133	154
49	Jan 30		Houston	2-1	W	19	28	2	40	135	155
50	Feb 1		Winnipeg	1-2	L	19	29	2	40	136	157
51	Feb 5		Québec	4-2	W	20	29	2	42	140	159
52	Feb 6	*	Houston	3-4	L	20	30	2	42	143	163

	date		opponent	score		w	l	t	pts	gf	ga
53	Feb 7		Cincinnati	5-1	W	21	30	2	44	148	164
54	Feb 11		Phoenix	2-1	W	22	30	2	46	150	165
55	Feb 13		Calgary	3-4	L-ot	22	31	2	46	153	169
56	Feb 14	*	Cincinnati	2-3	L	22	32	2	46	155	172
57	Feb 15		San Diego	2-3	L	22	33	2	46	157	175
58	Feb 19		New England	10-3	W	23	33	2	48	167	178
59	Feb 21	*	Cleveland	2-3	L	23	34	2	48	169	181
60	Feb 22		Phoenix	5-6	L	23	35	2	48	174	187
61	Feb 28	*	New England	4-4	T	23	35	3	49	178	191
62	Feb 29	*	Cincinnati	5-2	W	24	35	3	51	183	193
63	Mar 2	*	Phoenix	2-5	L	24	36	3	51	185	198
64	Mar 4		Cincinnati	3-1	W	25	36	3	53	188	199
65	Mar 6	*	Cincinnati	3-2	W	26	36	3	55	191	201
66	Mar 7		Cleveland	1-5	L	26	37	3	55	192	206
67	Mar 11		Toronto	3-1	W	27	37	3	57	195	207
68	Mar 12	*	Cincinnati	6-3	W	28	37	3	59	201	210
69	Mar 13		Phoenix	6-4	W	29	37	3	61	207	214
70	Mar 17	*	New England	5-2	W	30	37	3	63	212	216
71	Mar 18		San Diego	4-4	T	30	37	4	64	216	220
72	Mar 20	*	New England	1-1	T	30	37	5	65	217	221
73	Mar 23	*	San Diego	8-8	T	30	37	6	66	225	229
74	Mar 25		Houston	4-3	W-ot	31	37	6	68	229	232
75	Mar 26	*	Cleveland	3-2	W	32	37	6	70	232	234
76	Mar 28	*	New England	3-1	W	33	37	6	72	235	235
77	Apr 1		Houston	1-4	L	33	38	6	72	236	239
78	Apr 2	*	Toronto	3-1	W	34	38	6	74	239	240
79	Apr 3		New England	2-5	L	34	39	6	74	241	245
80	Apr 4	*	New England	4-2	W	35	39	6	76	245	247
			Second half record:			19	17	4	42	135	124

RECORD VS. OPPONENTS

opponent	season					home					away				
	w	l	t	gf	ga	w	l	t	gf	ga	w	l	t	gf	ga
Calgary	0	4	0	12	19	0	2	0	8	11	0	2	0	4	8
Cincinnati	8	3	0	38	25	5	1	0	21	11	3	2	0	17	14
Cleveland	5	5	0	28	31	3	2	0	14	16	2	3	0	14	15
Denver	1	3	0	14	13	0	2	0	6	10	1	1	0	8	3
Edmonton	1	3	0	10	15	1	1	0	5	6	0	2	0	5	9
Houston	3	4	0	17	20	3	1	0	11	8	0	3	0	6	12
Minnesota	0	4	0	14	20	0	2	0	6	8	0	2	0	8	12
New England	7	2	3	44	31	3	1	1	20	13	4	1	2	24	18
Phoenix	3	3	0	18	24	2	1	0	13	11	1	2	0	5	13
Québec	1	3	0	10	13	1	1	0	6	7	0	2	0	4	6
San Diego	0	3	3	17	23	0	2	1	6	9	0	1	2	11	14
Toronto	4	0	0	16	7	2	0	0	7	4	2	0	0	9	3
Winnipeg	2	2	0	7	6	1	1	0	4	3	1	1	0	3	3
TOTAL	35	39	6	245	247	21	17	2	127	117	14	22	4	118	130

RECORD BY MONTH

month	season					home					away				
	w	l	t	gf	ga	w	l	t	gf	ga	w	l	t	gf	ga
October	3	6	0	33	33	2	3	0	18	18	1	3	0	15	15
November	6	6	0	37	37	3	2	0	14	14	3	4	0	23	23
December	5	6	2	33	39	4	1	1	20	13	1	5	1	13	26
January	5	10	0	32	46	4	4	0	19	23	1	6	0	13	23
February	5	7	1	48	38	4	4	0	32	22	1	3	1	16	16
March	9	2	3	52	42	4	1	1	21	18	5	1	2	31	24
April	2	2	0	10	12	0	2	0	3	9	2	0	0	7	3
TOTAL	35	39	6	245	247	21	17	2	127	117	14	22	4	118	130

1976-1977 INDIANAPOLIS RACERS Game Results
Coach: Jacques Demers 36-37-8   (* away game)

	date		opponent	score		w	l	t	pts	gf	ga
1	Oct 8		Minnesota	4-3	W	1	0	0	2	4	3
2	Oct 10	*	Minnesota	1-4	L	1	1	0	2	5	7
3	Oct 15		Cincinnati	6-5	W-ot	2	1	0	4	11	12
4	Oct 17	*	Edmonton	2-7	L	2	2	0	4	13	19
5	Oct 19	*	Winnipeg	1-6	L	2	3	0	4	14	25
6	Oct 21	*	San Diego	4-4	T	2	3	1	5	18	29
7	Oct 23		Birmingham	1-3	L	2	4	1	5	19	32
8	Oct 27		San Diego	1-5	L	2	5	1	5	20	37
9	Oct 29		Québec	6-4	W	3	5	1	7	26	41
10	Nov 3	*	Cincinnati	2-8	L	3	6	1	7	28	49
11	Nov 4		Cincinnati	5-2	W	4	6	1	9	33	51
12	Nov 7	*	San Diego	0-3	L	4	7	1	9	33	54
13	Nov 9	*	Houston	2-7	L	4	8	1	9	35	61
14	Nov 10	*	Phoenix	3-3	T	4	8	2	10	38	64
15	Nov 13	*	Cincinnati	3-7	L	4	9	2	10	41	71
16	Nov 14	*	Québec	3-1	W	5	9	2	12	44	72
17	Nov 16		Cincinnati	5-3	W	6	9	2	14	49	75
18	Nov 19		Birmingham	4-0	W	7	9	2	16	53	75
19	Nov 20		Winnipeg	8-4	W	8	9	2	18	61	79
20	Nov 23		New England	4-3	W	9	9	2	20	65	82
21	Nov 24	*	Cincinnati	6-4	W	10	9	2	22	71	86
22	Nov 25		Québec	0-5	L	10	10	2	22	71	91
23	Nov 27	*	Québec	8-2	W	11	10	2	24	79	93
24	Nov 28	*	New England	4-3	W	12	10	2	26	83	96
25	Dec 2		Calgary	2-1	W	13	10	2	28	85	97
26	Dec 4		Edmonton	5-3	W	14	10	2	30	90	100
27	Dec 7	*	Birmingham	3-2	W-ot	15	10	2	32	93	102
28	Dec 10		San Diego	3-2	W	16	10	2	34	96	104
29	Dec 12		Houston	1-3	L	16	11	2	34	97	107
30	Dec 16		Minnesota	3-5	L	16	12	2	34	100	112
31	Dec 17	*	New England	5-4	W-ot	17	12	2	36	105	116
32	Dec 19		Birmingham	3-2	W-ot	18	12	2	38	108	118
33	Dec 26	*	San Diego	1-2	L	18	13	2	38	109	120
34	Dec 28	*	Phoenix	3-4	L	18	14	2	38	112	124
35	Jan 2		Phoenix	4-1	W	19	14	2	40	116	125
36	Jan 4	*	Winnipeg	1-2	L	19	15	2	40	117	127
37	Jan 8	*	Calgary	3-4	L	19	16	2	40	120	131
38	Jan 9	*	Edmonton	3-5	L	19	17	2	40	123	136
39	Jan 11	*	Calgary	4-3	W-ot	20	17	2	42	127	139
40	Jan 13		New England	4-1	W	21	17	2	44	131	140
			First half record:			21	17	2	44	131	140

	date		opponent	score		w	l	t	pts	gf	ga
41	Jan 14	*	Minnesota	5-9	L	21	18	2	44	136	149
42	Jan 15		Edmonton	6-3	W	22	18	2	46	142	152
43	Jan 21		Calgary	1-1	T	22	18	3	47	143	153
44	Jan 22	*	New England	3-3	T	22	18	4	48	146	156
45	Jan 23	*	Birmingham	2-6	L	22	19	4	48	148	162
46	Jan 25	*	Québec	1-2	L-ot	22	20	4	48	149	164
47	Jan 28		Québec	5-6	L	22	21	4	48	154	170
48	Jan 30		New England	5-0	W	23	21	4	50	159	170
49	Feb 1	*	Québec	4-5	L	23	22	4	50	163	175
50	Feb 2		Québec	6-5	W	24	22	4	52	169	180
51	Feb 5		Birmingham	5-2	W	25	22	4	54	174	182
52	Feb 6	*	New England	5-5	T	25	22	5	55	179	187

	date		opponent	score		w	l	t	pts	gf	ga
53	Feb 8		Houston	4-4	T	25	22	6	56	183	191
54	Feb 9	*	Cincinnati	0-9	L	25	23	6	56	183	200
55	Feb 11		Québec	1-5	L	25	24	6	56	184	205
56	Feb 12	*	New England	5-1	W	26	24	6	58	189	206
57	Feb 13		Winnipeg	5-7	L	26	25	6	58	194	213
58	Feb 17	*	Winnipeg	2-4	L	26	26	6	58	196	217
59	Feb 19		Phoenix	5-6	L	26	27	6	58	201	223
60	Feb 20	*	Birmingham	2-2	T	26	27	7	59	203	225
61	Feb 22	*	Québec	2-4	L	26	28	7	59	205	229
62	Feb 25	*	Edmonton	3-2	W	27	28	7	61	208	231
63	Feb 27	*	Calgary	1-2	L	27	29	7	61	209	233
64	Mar 4		San Diego	7-4	W	28	29	7	63	216	237
65	Mar 5	*	Cincinnati	0-6	L	28	30	7	63	216	243
66	Mar 6		Phoenix	3-2	W-ot	29	30	7	65	219	245
67	Mar 10		Edmonton	3-4	L	29	31	7	65	222	249
68	Mar 12		Birmingham	7-2	W	30	31	7	67	229	251
69	Mar 13	*	Houston	0-5	L	30	32	7	67	229	256
70	Mar 15		Calgary	3-1	W	31	32	7	69	232	257
71	Mar 17	*	Birmingham	5-2	W	32	32	7	71	237	259
72	Mar 18		Winnipeg	5-7	L	32	33	7	71	242	266
73	Mar 20		Houston	3-8	L	32	34	7	71	245	274
74	Mar 22		Cincinnati	3-1	W	33	34	7	73	248	275
75	Mar 24		Québec	4-3	W	34	34	7	75	252	278
76	Mar 26	*	New England	4-2	W	35	34	7	77	256	280
77	Mar 27	*	Birmingham	3-7	L	35	35	7	77	259	287
78	Mar 30		Cincinnati	5-5	T	35	35	8	78	264	292
79	Apr 2		New England	2-3	L-ot	35	36	8	78	266	295
80	Apr 3	*	Houston	7-3	W	36	36	8	80	273	298
81	Apr 6	*	Phoenix	3-7	L	36	37	8	80	276	305
			Second half record:			15	20	6	36	145	165

RECORD VS. OPPONENTS

	season					home					away				
opponent	w	l	t	gf	ga	w	l	t	gf	ga	w	l	t	gf	ga
Birmingham	6	3	1	35	28	4	1	0	20	9	2	2	1	15	19
Calgary	3	2	1	14	12	2	0	1	6	3	1	2	0	8	9
Cincinnati	5	4	1	35	50	4	0	1	24	16	1	4	0	11	34
Edmonton	3	3	0	22	24	2	1	0	14	10	1	2	0	8	14
Houston	1	4	1	14	30	0	2	1	8	15	1	2	0	9	15
Minnesota	1	3	0	13	21	1	1	0	7	8	0	2	0	6	13
New England	7	1	2	41	25	3	1	0	15	7	4	0	2	26	18
Phoenix	2	3	1	21	23	2	1	0	12	9	0	2	1	9	14
Québec	5	6	0	40	42	3	3	0	22	28	2	3	0	18	14
San Diego	2	3	0	16	20	2	1	0	11	11	0	2	1	5	9
Winnipeg	1	5	0	22	30	1	2	0	18	18	0	3	0	4	12
TOTAL	36	37	8	276	305	24	13	3	157	134	12	24	5	119	171

RECORD BY MONTH

	season					home					away				
month	w	l	t	gf	ga	w	l	t	gf	ga	w	l	t	gf	ga
October	3	5	1	26	41	3	2	0	18	20	0	3	1	8	21
November	9	5	1	57	55	5	1	0	26	17	4	4	1	31	38
December	6	4	0	29	28	4	2	0	17	16	2	2	0	12	12
January	5	7	2	47	46	4	1	1	25	12	1	6	1	22	34
February	4	8	3	50	63	2	3	1	26	29	2	5	2	24	34
March	8	6	1	55	59	6	3	1	43	37	2	3	0	12	22
April	1	2	0	12	13	0	1	0	2	3	1	1	0	10	1
TOTAL	36	37	8	276	305	24	13	3	157	134	12	24	5	119	171

1977-1978 INDIANAPOLIS RACERS Game Results
Coaches: Ron Ingram 16-31-4; Bill Goldsworthy 8-20-1 (* away game)

	date		opponent	score		w	l	t	pts	gf	ga
1	Oct 12	*	Cincinnati	5-4	W	1	0	0	2	5	4
2	Oct 15	*	Houston	1-5	L	1	1	0	2	6	9
3	Oct 16	*	Winnipeg	1-9	L	1	2	0	2	7	18
4	Oct 18		New England	2-2	T	1	2	1	3	9	20
5	Oct 21		Québec	4-4	T	1	2	2	4	13	24
6	Oct 25	*	Birmingham	5-4	W	2	2	2	6	18	28
7	Oct 26		Winnipeg	5-3	W	3	2	2	8	23	31
8	Oct 29		Birmingham	6-2	W	4	2	2	10	29	33
9	Nov 1		Houston	6-3	W	5	2	2	12	35	36
10	Nov 4	*	Edmonton	1-3	L	5	3	2	12	36	39
11	Nov 11	*	Houston	3-5	L	5	4	2	12	39	44
12	Nov 12	*	New England	3-5	L	5	5	2	12	42	49
13	Nov 15		New England	4-6	L	5	6	2	12	46	55
14	Nov 18		Birmingham	1-2	L	5	7	2	12	47	57
15	Nov 19	*	Winnipeg	4-6	L	5	8	2	12	51	63
16	Nov 20	*	Québec	2-5	L	5	9	2	12	53	68
17	Nov 23	*	New England	3-3	T	5	9	3	13	56	71
18	Nov 24		Edmonton	5-4	W- ot	6	9	3	15	61	75
19	Nov 26		Cincinnati	5-7	L	6	10	3	15	66	82
20	Nov 30	*	Cincinnati	0-3	L	6	11	3	15	66	85
21	Dec 1		Québec	5-4	W	7	11	3	17	71	89
22	Dec 2	*	Houston	4-2	W	8	11	3	19	75	91
23	Dec 4	*	Birmingham	0-3	L	8	12	3	19	75	94
24	Dec 6		New England	5-2	W	9	12	3	21	80	96
25	Dec 9		Czechoslovakia	3-5	L	9	13	3	21	83	101
26	Dec 10	*	Québec	3-5	L	9	14	3	21	86	106
27	Dec 11	*	Winnipeg	1-7	L	9	15	3	21	87	113
28	Dec 14	*	Cincinnati	1-3	L	9	16	3	21	88	116
29	Dec 15		Houston	3-3	T	9	16	4	22	91	119
30	Dec 18		Soviet All-Stars	3-4	L	9	17	4	22	94	123
31	Dec 22		Cincinnati	1-4	L	9	18	4	22	95	127
32	Dec 23	*	New England	3-5	L	9	19	4	22	98	132
33	Dec 28	*	Cincinnati	4-5	L- ot	9	20	4	22	102	137
34	Dec 29		Houston	1-7	L	9	21	4	22	103	144
35	Dec 30	*	Edmonton	5-8	L	9	22	4	22	108	152
36	Jan 4		Birmingham	4-1	W	10	22	4	24	112	153
37	Jan 6		New England	4-3	W	11	22	4	26	116	156
38	Jan 7	*	Houston	2-1	W	12	22	4	28	118	157
39	Jan 8	*	Winnipeg	2-4	L	12	23	4	28	120	161
40	Jan 11		Québec	2-1	W	13	23	4	30	122	162
			First half record:			13	23	4	30	122	162
	date		opponent	score		w	l	t	pts	gf	ga
41	Jan 14		Winnipeg	3-6	L	13	24	4	30	125	168
42	Jan 20		Houston	3-4	L	13	25	4	30	128	172
43	Jan 21		Edmonton	2-3	L	13	26	4	30	130	175
44	Jan 22	*	Winnipeg	5-4	W	14	26	4	32	135	179
45	Jan 25	*	Edmonton	2-6	L	14	27	4	32	137	185
46	Jan 30		Cincinnati	3-4	L	14	28	4	32	140	189
47	Jan 31		Edmonton	4-6	L	14	29	4	32	144	195
48	Feb 1	*	Cincinnati	0-8	L	14	30	4	32	144	203
49	Feb 3		Québec	5-4	W- ot	15	30	4	34	149	207
50	Feb 4	*	Birmingham	2-5	L	15	31	4	34	151	212
51	Feb 5		Birmingham	6-1	W	16	31	4	36	157	213
52	Feb 11		Winnipeg	3-5	L	16	31	4	36	160	218

	date		opponent	score		w	l	t	pts	gf	ga
53	Feb 15		Québec	9-6	W	17	32	4	38	169	224
54	Feb 17	*	Birmingham	4-5	L-ot	17	33	4	38	173	229
55	Feb 18		New England	1-4	L	17	34	4	38	174	233
56	Feb 19	*	Edmonton	3-4	L	17	35	4	38	177	237
57	Feb 25	*	Québec	5-7	L	17	36	4	38	182	244
58	Feb 26	*	Birmingham	6-3	W	18	36	4	40	188	247
59	Mar 1		Houston	5-1	W	19	36	4	42	193	248
60	Mar 3	*	Edmonton	8-6	W	20	36	4	44	201	254
61	Mar 4		Winnipeg	8-6	W	21	36	4	46	209	260
62	Mar 5		Cincinnati	4-2	W	22	36	4	48	213	262
63	Mar 8		Québec	4-5	L-ot	22	37	4	48	217	267
64	Mar 9	*	Winnipeg	5-6	L	22	38	4	48	222	273
65	Mar 11		Houston	4-2	W	23	38	4	50	226	275
66	Mar 12	*	Houston	3-6	L	23	39	4	50	229	281
67	Mar 15	*	New England	0-7	L	23	40	4	50	229	288
68	Mar 16	*	Québec	2-5	L	23	41	4	50	231	293
69	Mar 18	*	Cincinnati	2-4	L	23	42	4	50	233	297
70	Mar 19	*	Birmingham	3-3	T	23	42	5	51	236	300
71	Mar 21	*	New England	3-6	L	23	43	5	51	239	306
72	Mar 24	*	Edmonton	0-4	L	23	44	5	51	239	310
73	Mar 28		Edmonton	3-4	L-ot	23	45	5	51	242	314
74	Mar 30		Winnipeg	1-4	L	23	46	5	51	243	318
75	Apr 1		Edmonton	1-4	L	23	47	5	51	244	322
76	Apr 2		Cincinnati	6-3	W	24	47	5	53	250	325
77	Apr 7		Cincinnati	4-6	L	24	48	5	53	254	331
78	Apr 8	*	Québec	3-7	L	24	49	5	53	257	338
79	Apr 9		Birmingham	7-9	L	24	50	5	53	264	347
80	Apr 11	*	New England	3-6	L	24	51	5	53	267	353
			Second half record:			11	28	1	23	145	191

RECORD VS. OPPONENTS

month	season					home					away				
	w	l	t	gf	ga	w	l	t	gf	ga	w	l	t	gf	ga
Birmingham	5	5	1	44	38	3	2	0	24	15	2	3	1	20	23
Cincinnati	3	9	0	35	53	2	4	0	23	26	1	5	0	12	27
Edmonton	2	9	0	34	52	1	4	0	15	21	1	5	0	19	31
Houston	5	5	1	35	39	3	2	1	22	20	2	3	0	13	19
New England	2	7	2	31	49	2	2	1	16	17	0	5	1	15	32
Québec	4	6	1	44	53	4	1	1	29	24	0	5	0	15	29
Winnipeg	3	8	0	38	60	2	4	0	24	300	1	4	0	14	30
Touring Teams	0	2	0	6	9	0	2	0	6	9	-	-	-	-	-
TOTAL	24	51	5	267	353	17	21	3	159	162	7	30	2	108	191

RECORD BY MONTH

month	season					home					away				
	w	l	t	gf	ga	w	l	t	gf	ga	w	l	t	gf	ga
October	4	2	2	29	33	2	0	2	17	11	2	2	0	12	22
November	2	9	1	37	52	2	4	0	25	28	0	5	1	12	24
December	3	11	1	42	67	2	4	1	21	29	1	7	0	21	38
January	5	7	0	36	43	3	5	0	25	28	2	2	0	11	15
February	4	7	0	44	52	3	2	0	24	20	1	5	0	20	32
March	5	10	1	55	71	4	3	0	29	24	1	7	1	26	47
April	1	5	0	24	35	1	3	0	18	22	0	2	0	6	13
TOTAL	24	51	5	267	353	17	21	3	159	162	7	30	2	108	191

1978-1979 INDIANAPOLIS RACERS Game Results
Coach: Pat Stapleton 5-18-2   (* away game)

	date		opponent	score		w	l	t	pts	gf	ga
1	Oct 14		Winnipeg	3-6	L	0	1	0	0	3	6
2	Oct 15		Birmingham	3-9	L	0	2	0	0	6	15
3	Oct 18	*	Québec	4-0	W	1	2	0	2	10	15
4	Oct 20		Edmonton	3-4	L	1	3	0	2	13	19
5	Oct 22		New England	3-6	L	1	4	0	2	16	25
6	Oct 27	*	Birmingham	2-4	L	1	5	0	2	18	29
7	Oct 28		Winnipeg	3-2	W	2	5	0	4	21	31
8	Oct 29	*	Winnipeg	3-3	T	2	5	1	5	24	34
9	Nov 3	*	New England	3-6	L	2	6	1	5	27	40
10	Nov 4		New England	6-6	T	2	6	2	6	33	46
11	Nov 5	*	Winnipeg	2-6	L	2	7	2	6	35	52
12	Nov 8	*	Cincinnati	0-4	L	2	8	2	6	35	56
13	Nov 11	*	Québec	2-8	L	2	9	2	6	37	64
14	Nov 17	*	Edmonton	1-6	L	2	10	2	6	38	70
15	Nov 19	*	Winnipeg	2-5	L	2	11	2	6	40	75
16	Nov 23		Winnipeg	1-5	L	2	12	2	6	41	80
17	Nov 24	*	Cincinnati	5-8	L	2	13	2	6	46	88
18	Nov 25		Cincinnati	6-3	W	3	13	2	8	52	91
19	Nov 28	*	Edmonton	2-8	L	3	14	2	8	54	99
20	Dec 1		Birmingham	6-3	W	4	14	2	10	60	102
21	Dec 2	*	Birmingham	2-4	L	4	15	2	10	62	106
22	Dec 3		Cincinnati	2-4	L	4	16	2	10	64	110
23	Dec 7		Winnipeg	4-9	L	4	17	2	10	68	119
24	Dec 10		Edmonton	6-4	W	5	17	2	12	74	123
25	Dec 12		New England	4-7	L	5	18	2	12	78	130

Franchise folds December 15, 1978

RECORD VS. OPPONENTS

season	season					home					away				
opponent	w	l	t	gf	ga	w	l	t	gf	ga	w	l	t	gf	ga
Birmingham	1	3	0	13	20	1	1	0	9	12	0	2	0	4	8
Cincinnati	1	3	0	13	19	1	1	0	8	7	0	2	0	5	12
Edmonton	1	3	0	12	22	1	1	0	9	8	0	2	0	3	14
New England	0	3	1	16	25	0	2	1	13	19	0	1	0	3	6
Québec	1	1	0	6	8	-	-	-	-	-	1	1	0	6	8
Winnipeg	1	5	1	18	36	1	3	0	11	22	0	2	1	7	14
TOTAL	5	18	2	78	130	4	8	1	50	68	1	10	1	28	62

RECORD BY MONTH

season	season					home					away				
month	w	l	t	gf	ga	w	l	t	gf	ga	w	l	t	gf	ga
October	2	5	1	24	34	1	4	0	15	27	1	1	1	9	7
November	1	9	1	30	65	1	1	1	13	14	0	8	0	17	51
December	2	4	0	24	31	2	3	0	22	27	0	1	0	2	4
TOTAL	5	18	2	78	130	4	8	1	50	68	1	10	1	28	62

RACERS SEASON-BY-SEASON SCORING

gp = games played; g = goals; a = assists; pts = points; pim = penalties in minutes;
ppg = power play goals; shg = short handed goals; +/- plus/minus record;
sog = shots on goal; sc% = scoring percentage. An asterisk (*) in front of a name indicates a player finished the season with another team; the destination team is noted with (>). The symbol (<) indicates the player started the season with another team.

1974-1975 — Regular Season

pos	no.	name		gp	g	a	pts	pim	ppg	shg	sog	sc%
RW	17	*Andrascik, Steve	> M-B	20	2	4	6	16			56	0.036
D	3	Ash, Bob		64	1	14	15	19			53	0.019
D	24	Block, Ken	< SD	37	0	17	17	18	0	0	48	0.000
LW	21	Bond, Kerry		71	22	15	37	23			204	0.108
RW	19	*Bredin, Gary	> M-B	10	3	2	5	8			12	0.250
G	1	Brown, Andy		52	0	1	1	75	0	0	0	-
C	9	Buchanan, Ron	< Cle, Edm	32	16	15	31	16	9		89	0.180
D	23	Cote, Roger		36	0	6	6	24	0	0	33	0.000
D	2	Desjardine, Ken		46	0	8	8	68	0	0	60	0.000
G		Dion, Michel		1	0	0	0	0	0	0	0	-
G	31	Dyck, Ed		32	0	0	0	6	0	0	0	-
C	16	Fitchner, Bob		78	11	19	30	96			108	0.102
D	5	Fraser, Rick		4	0	0	0	2	0	0	5	0.000
D	4	Hanmer, Craig		27	1	0	1	15			28	0.036
RW	10	Harbaruk, Nick		78	20	23	43	52			157	0.127
C	12	*Hardy, Joe	< Chi, > SD	32	2	17	19	36			64	0.031
D	6	*Hargreaves, Jim	> SD	37	2	5	7	30			63	0.032
RW	26	Heatley, Murray	< Min	29	15	8	23	25			83	0.181
D	18	Hopiavuori, Ralph		28	2	8	10	21			64	0.031
D	25	Horton, Bill		59	2	9	11	30			42	0.048
C	15	Johnson, Jim	< Min	42	7	15	22	12			62	0.112
D	8	Kannegiesser, Gord		4	1	4	5	4			6	0.167
D	26	*Kennett, Murray	> Edm	28	1	3	4	8			9	0.111
C	8	Locas, Jacques	< M-B	11	0	1	1	2	0	0	8	0.000
RW	20	McDonald, Brian	< M-B	47	14	15	29	19			104	0.135
LW	12	McKenzie, Brian		9	1	0	1	6			9	0.111
D	19	Proceviat, Dick	< Chi	52	1	28	29	51			65	0.015
LW	27	Pumple, Rich		34	4	8	12	29			72	0.056
C	8	*Richardson, Steve	> M-B	19	1	4	5	16			39	0.026
C	15	*Robertson, Joe	> M-B	18	4	4	8	23			31	0.129
C	22	Sheridan, John		58	17	11	28	20			137	0.124
C	17	Sicinski, Bob		77	19	34	53	12		2	206	0.092
LW	9	Smith, Ross		15	1	6	7	19			23	0.043
RW	11	Walters, Ron		17	2	1	3	9			18	0.111
C	7	Whitlock, Bobby		73	31	26	57	56			290	0.107
C	14	Wiste, Jim		75	13	28	41	30			114	0.114
D	5	Woytowich, Bob	< Wpg	42	0	8	8	28	0	0	30	0.000

1974-75 Regular Season Goaltending

	gp	min	ga	en	sho	w	l	t	gaa	sa	sv%
Brown, Andy	52	2979	206	1	2	15	35	0	4.15	1627	.873
Dion, Michel	1	59	4	0	0	0	1	0	4.07	38	.895
Dyck, Ed	32	1692	123	4	0	3	21	3	4.36	913	.865
TEAM TOTALS	78	4730	333	5	2	18	57	3	4.26		

RACERS SEASON-BY-SEASON SCORING (continued)

1975-1976   **Regular Season**

pos	no.	name		gp	g	a	pts	pim	+/-	ppg	shg	sog	sc%
D	5	Baltimore, Bryon	< D-O	37	1	10	11	30	+8	0	0	44	0.023
D	24	Block, Ken		79	1	25	26	28	+4	0	0	104	0.010
LW	21	Bond, Kerry		15	2	0	2	9	-7	0	0	20	0.100
G	1	Brown, Andy		24	0	3	3	17		0	0	0	-
C	9	Buchanan, Ron		23	4	7	11	4	-5	1	0	60	0.067
D	4	Clackson, Kim		77	1	12	13	351	-10	1	0	71	0.014
ILW	18	Coates, Brian		59	11	16	27	24	-5	2	1	72	0.153
D		Critch, Glen		3	0	0	0	0	0	0	0	0	-
G	31	Dion, Michel		31	0	0	0	2		0	0	0	-
D	25	*Dubois, Michel	> Que	34	2	2	4	104	-11	1	0	29	0.069
C	16	*Fitchner, Bob	> Que	52	15	16	31	112	0	5	0	74	0.203
RW	10	Harbaruk, Nick		76	23	19	42	26	+10	2	2	170	0.135
C	7	Harris, Hugh	< Cgy	41	12	28	40	23	+1	3	0	166	0.072
RW	26	Heatley, Murray		34	2	5	7	7	-7	0	0	46	0.043
G	30	Holmquist, Leif		19	0	0	0	4		0	0	0	-
LW		Jones, Bob		2	0	0	0	0	-1	0	0	3	0.000
C	15	Karlander, Al		79	16	28	44	36	+15	4	0	121	0.132
C	6	Keon, Dave	< Min	12	3	7	10	2	+2	1	0	40	0.075
IRW	8	LeClerc, Rene	< Que	40	18	21	39	52	+1	7	0	152	0.118
RW	25	Lomenda, Mark	< D-O	2	0	0	0	0	-1	0	0	4	0.000
RW	14	MacDonald, Blair	< Edm	56	19	11	30	14	+2	1	0	142	0.134
D	2	Maggs, Darryl	< D-O	36	5	16	21	40	+5	1	0	90	0.056
RW	11	McDonald, Brian		63	16	17	33	58	-6	1	2	117	0.137
C	16	Parizeau, Michel	< Que	23	13	15	28	20	+9	8	0	58	0.224
G	28	Park, Jim		11	0	1	1	2		0	0	0	-
D	2	*Prentice, Bill	> Que	38	4	2	6	92	-5	0	0	47	0.085
D	3	Proceviat, Dick		73	7	13	20	31	+7	0	0	65	0.108
LW	19	Rochon, Francois	< D-O	19	6	2	8	31	0	2	0	21	0.286
LW		Roselle, Bob		1	0	0	0	0	-1	0	0	1	0.000
RW	20	Scharf, Ted		74	7	13	20	56	-8	2	0	90	0.078
C	22	Sheridan, John		11	1	2	3	0	-5	0	0	9	0.111
C	17	Sicinski, Bob		70	9	34	43	4	-2	3	0	140	0.064
D	12	Stapleton, Pat		80	5	40	45	48	-7	3	0	205	0.024
LW	8/21	Thomas, Reg		80	23	17	40	23	+1	4	0	192	0.120
C	7	Whitlock, Bobby		30	7	15	22	16	+1	2	0	111	0.063
C	14	Wiste, Jim		7	0	2	2	0	-2	0	0	3	0.000
D	5	Woytowich, Bob		42	1	7	8	14	0	0	0	23	0.043
C	6	Wyrozub, Randy		55	11	14	25	8	-4	5	1	79	0.139

1975-76 Regular Season Goaltending

	gp	min	ga	en	sho	w	l	t	gaa	sa	sv%%
Brown, Andy	24	1368	82	0	1	9	11	2	3.60	751	.891
Dion, Michel	31	1860	85	1	0	14	15	1	2.74	942	.910
Holmquist, Leif	19	1079	54	2	0	6	9	3	3.00	522	.897
Park, Jim	11	572	23	0	0	6	4	0	2.41	297	.923
TEAM TOTALS	80	4879	244	3	1	35	39	6	3.00		

RACERS SEASON-BY-SEASON SCORING (continued)

1976-1977 Regular Season

pos	no.	name		gp	g	a	pts	pim	+/-	ppg	shg	sog	sc%
D	5	Baltimore, Bryon		55	0	15	15	63	-22	0	0	37	0.000
D	24	Block, Ken		52	3	10	13	25	-12	0	0	34	0.088
G	1	Brown, Andy		10	0	0	0	0		0	0	0	-
G	1	Burchell, Randy		5	0	1	1	0		0	0	0	-
C	21	*Campbell, Bryan	>Edm	8	1	4	5	6	-8	1	0	21	0.048
D	4	Clackson, Kim		71	3	8	11	168	-9	0	0	44	0.068
LW	18	Coates, Brian		16	1	5	6	4	-2	0	0	24	0.042
G	31	Dion, Michel		42	0	0	0	0		0	0	0	-
RW	20	Harbaruk, Nick		27	2	2	4	2	-16	0	0	28	0.071
C	7	Harris, Hugh		46	21	35	56	21	+10	4	4	182	0.115
G	30	Hoganson, Paul	<Cin	11	0	0	0	2		0	0	0	-
D	10	Inkpen, Dave	<Cin	32	4	12	16	20	+10	0	0	43	0.093
C	15	Karlander, Al		65	17	28	45	23	+5	4	0	98	0.173
RW	8	LeClerc, Rene		68	25	30	55	43	-7	2	0	174	0.144
RW	25	Lomenda, Mark		56	9	12	21	14	-11	0	0	99	0.091
RW	14	MacDonald, Blair		81	34	30	64	28	+10	8	0	253	0.134
C	6	*MacGregor, Gary	>NE	16	0	5	5	4	-11	0	0	33	0.000
D	2	Maggs, Darryl		81	16	55	71	114	+4	5	1	310	0.052
D	21	Mavety, Larry		10	2	2	4	8	-1	0	0	13	0.154
RW	11	McDonald, Brian		50	15	13	28	48	-20	5	2	89	0.169
RW	6	Paiement, Rosaire	<NE	67	18	25	43	91	-3	2	0	144	0.125
G	28	Park, Jim		31	0	1	1	6		0	0	0	-
C	16	Parizeau, Michel		75	18	37	55	39	+6	8	0	139	0.129
LW	22	Peacosh, Gene	<Edm	64	22	26	48	21	-1	6	0	124	0.177
D	3	Proceviat, Dick		55	2	12	14	33	-7	0	0	65	0.031
LW	19	Rochon, Francois		67	15	8	23	8	-13	2	0	122	0.123
C	17	Sicinski, Bob		60	12	24	36	14	-8	1	0	141	0.085
D	12	Stapleton, Pat		81	8	45	53	29	-28	4	0	156	0.051
LW	9	Thomas, Reg		79	25	30	55	34	-9	5	0	241	0.104
C	23	Zuke, Mike		15	3	4	7	2	-2	0	0	24	0.125

1976-77 Regular Season Goaltending

	gp	min	ga	en	sho	w	l	t	gaa	sa	sv%
Brown, Andy	10	430	26	0	0	1	4	1	3.63	195	.867
Burchell, Randy	5	136	8	0	0	1	0	0	3.53	89	.910
Dion, Michel	42	2286	128	4	1	17	19	3	3.36	1174	.891
Hoganson, Paul < Cin	11	395	24	0	0	3	2	0	3.65	199	.879
Park, Jim	31	1727	114	1	1	14	12	4	3.96	898	.873
TEAM TOTALS	81	4974	300	5	2	36	37	8	3.62		

RACERS SEASON-BY-SEASON SCORING (continued)

1977-1978   Regular Season

pos	no.	name		gp	g	a	pts	pim	+/-	ppg	shg	sog	sc%
C	26	Adduono, Ray		8	1	2	3	0	-5	0	0	10	0.100
D	5	*Baltimore, Bryon	> Cin	22	1	7	8	47	0	0	0	14	0.071
D	25	Blackwood, Bill		3	0	0	0	0		0	0	4	0.000
D	24	Block, Ken		77	1	25	26	34	-39	1	0	30	0.033
LW	15	Burgess, Don		79	11	12	23	2	-30	2	0	100	0.110
LW	26	Constantin, Charles	< Que	6	2	1	3	0	+1	2	0	7	0.286
LW	12	Devine, Kevin		76	19	23	42	141	-24	1	0	143	0.133
D	26	Dornseif, Dave		3	0	1	1	0	+1	0	0	1	0.000
LW	23	Driscoll, Peter	< Que	56	25	21	46	130	0	5	0	122	0.205
D	22	Fortier, Dave		54	1	15	16	86	-17	0	0	69	0.014
LW	11	French, John		74	9	8	17	6	-25	2	2	67	0.134
RW	19	Goldsworthy, Bill		32	8	10	18	10	+2	0	0	51	0.157
C	7	*Harris, Hugh	> Cin	19	1	7	8	6	-4	0	0	23	0.043
D	2	Inkpen, Dave	<Edm, Que	24	1	9	10	24	-5	0	0	26	0.038
G	30	Inness, Gary		52	0	0	0	42		0	0	0	-
D	3	Irwin, Glen	< Hou	20	0	0	0	72		0	0		-
LW	9	Larose, Claude	< Cin	28	14	16	30	12	-15	3	0	68	0.206
RW	8	LeClerc, Rene		60	12	15	27	31	-7	2	0	110	0.109
C	10	Leduc, Richie	< Cin	28	10	15	25	38	-16	3	0	70	0.143
D	2	*Maggs, Darryl	> Cin	51	6	15	21	30	-27	3	0	116	0.052
D	5	Marotte, Gilles	< Cin	44	2	13	15	18	-17	0	0	49	0.041
G	1	McDuffe, Pete		12	0	0	0	0		0	0	0	-
G	31	Mio, Ed		17	0	0	0	0		0	0	0	-
D	4	Morrison, Kevin		75	17	40	57	49	-32	6	1	206	0.083
RW	6	Paiement, Rosaire		61	6	24	30	81	-13	1	0	84	0.071
C	16	Parizeau, Michel		70	13	27	40	47	-13	2	0	75	0.173
G	28	Park, Jim		12	0	0	0	6		0	0	0	-
RW	17	Patenaude, Rusty		73	23	19	42	71	-20	1	0	197	0.117
C	21	*Powis, Lynn	> Wpg	14	4	6	10	2	-5	0	0	34	0.118
D	21	Prentice, Bill		71	1	1	2	28	-4	0	0	28	0.036
C	10	Rhiness, Brad		12	3	3	6	12	-4	0	0	14	0.214
LW	20	St. Sauveur, Claude		72	36	42	78	24	-5	7	0	218	0.165
C	18	Sheehan, Bobby		29	8	7	15	6	-19	1	3	70	0.114
LW	26	Smedsmo, Dale		6	0	3	3	7	+3	0	0	9	0.000
RW	19	Spring, Frank		13	2	4	6	2	+1	1	0	20	0.100
RW	7	Stoughton, Blaine	< Cin	47	13	13	26	28	-24	5	0	102	0.127
LW	9	*Thomas, Reg	> Cin	49	15	16	31	44	-11	7	0	120	0.125
D	14	Wilkins, Barry		79	2	21	23	79	-35	1	0	89	0.022

1977-78 Regular Season Goaltending

	gp	min	ga	en	sho	w	l	t	gaa	sa	sv%
Inness, Gary	52	2850	200	6	0	14	30	4	4.21	1543	.870
McDuffe, Peter	12	539	39	1	0	1	6	1	4.34	313	.875
Mio, Ed	17	900	64	1	0	6	8	0	4.27	470	.864
Park, Jim	12	589	41	1	0	3	7	0	4.21	323	.873
TEAM TOTALS	80	4878	344	9	0	24	51	5	4.23		

RACERS SEASON-BY-SEASON SCORING (continued)

1978-1979　　　　　Regular Season

pos	no.	name		gp	g	a	pts	pim	+/-	ppg	shg	sog	sc%
D	5	*Baltimore, Bryon	> Cin	2	1	1	2	2	-1	0	0	4	0.250
D	24	Block, Ken		22	2	3	5	10	-11	0	0	9	0.222
LW	15	Burgess, Don		3	1	1	2	0	-4	0	0	3	0.333
LW	23	*Driscoll, Peter	> Edm	8	3	1	4	17	1	1	0	23	0.130
LW	14	*George, Wes	> Edm	9	4	2	6	23	-11	1	0	13	0.308
LW	17	Greig, Bruce		21	3	7	10	64	-5	0	0	13	0.231
C	99	*Gretzky, Wayne	> Edm	8	3	3	6	0	-3	0	0	17	0.176
D	21	*Hughes, John	> Edm	22	3	4	7	48	-16	0	0	24	0.125
D	2	*Inkpen, Dave	> NE	25	1	8	9	22	-5	0	0	34	0.029
G	30	Inness, Gary		10	0	0	0	9		0	0	0	0.000
D	3	Irwin, Glenn		24	0	1	1	124	-10	0	0	19	0.000
LW	9	Larose, Claude		13	5	8	13	0	+5	0	0	34	0.147
RW	27	Larway, Don		25	8	10	18	39	-20	2	0	56	0.143
RW	8	*LeClerc, Rene	> Que	22	5	7	12	12	+2	1	0	54	0.093
C	10	*Leduc, Richie	> Que	13	5	9	14	14	-2	2	0	68	0.074
LW	26	Leroux, Gerry		10	0	3	3	2	-4	0	0	13	0.000
C	11	MacGregor, Gary		17	8	4	12	0	-12	1	0	45	0.178
LW	10	Magee, Dean		5	0	1	1	10	-2	0	0	6	0.000
D	6	McLeod, Al		25	0	11	11	22	0	0	0	23	0.000
C	18	*Messier, Mark	> Cin	5	0	0	0	0	-4	0	0	7	0.000
G	31	*Mio, Ed	> Edm	5	0	1	1	2		0	0	0	0.000
C	25	Moretto, Angelo		18	3	1	4	2	-6	1	0	12	0.250
D	4	*Morrison, Kevin	> Que	5	0	2	2	0	-10	0	0	10	0.000
C	18	Morrow, Dave		10	2	10	12	29	-13	0	0	15	0.133
RW	12	Nugent, Kevin		25	2	8	10	20	-2	0	0	38	0.053
C	16	*Parizeau, Michel	> Cin	22	4	9	13	4	-1	0	0	25	0.160
D	5	Rollins, Jerry		7	0	1	1	7	-4	0	0	4	0.000
D	4	Sacharuk, Larry		16	2	9	11	25	-11	2	0	49	0.041
LW	20	*St. Sauveur, Claude	> Cin	17	4	2	6	12	-6	2	0	38	0.105
G	1	*Smith, Gary	> Wpg	11	0	0	0	0		0	0	0	0.000
RW	7	*Stoughton, Blaine	> NE	25	9	9	18	16	-18	3	0	78	0.115

1978-79 Regular Season Goaltending

	gp	min	ga	en	sho	w	l	t	gaa	sa	sv%
Inness, Gary	10	609	51	1	0	3	6	1	5.02	369	.862
Mio, Ed > Edm	5	242	13	0	1	2	2	0	3.22	153	.915
Smith, Gary > Wpg	11	664	61	4	0	0	10	1	5.51	400	.848
TEAM TOTALS	**25**	**1515**	**125**	**5**	**1**	**5**	**18**	**2**	**4.95**		

1975-1976 Playoff Scoring

pos	no.	name		gp	g	a	pts	pim	+/-
D	5	Baltimore, Bryon	< D-O	7	0	1	1	4	0
LW	21	Bond, Kerry		7	1	0	1	11	0
D	4	Clackson, Kim		6	0	0	0	25	-2
ILW	18	Coates, Brian		4	0	0	0	6	-2
G	31	Dion, Michel		3	0	0	0	0	
RW	10	Harbaruk, Nick		7	2	0	2	10	+2
C	7	Harris, Hugh	< Cgy	7	2	5	7	8	-3
C	15	Karlander, Al		3	0	0	0	4	0
C	6	Keon, Dave	< Min	7	2	2	4	2	0
IRW	8	LeClerc, Rene	< Que	7	2	5	7	7	-3
RW	14	MacDonald, Blair	< Edm	567	0	0	0	0	-3
D	2	Maggs, Darryl	< D-O	7	1	0	1	20	-2
RW	11	McDonald, Brian		7	0	1	1	12	-1
C	16	Parizeau, Michel	< Que	237	4	4	8	6	-3
G	28	Park, Jim		6	0	0	0	0	
D	3	Proceviat, Dick		7	0	0	0	2	-3
RW	20	Scharf, Ted		7	0	0	0	5	0
C	17	Sicinski, Bob		7	0	0	0	2	-1
D	12	Stapleton, Pat		7	0	2	2	2	-3
LW	8/21	Thomas, Reg		7	1	0	1	4	-1

1975-76 Playoff Goaltending

	gp	min	ga	en	sho	w	l	gaa
Dion, Michel	3	126	5	-	0	0	2	2.38
Park, Jim	6	293	12	-	2	3	2	2.45
TEAM TOTALS	7	419	17	1	2	3	4	2.43

1976-1977 Playoff Scoring

pos	no.	name		gp	g	a	pts	pim	+/-
D	5	Baltimore, Bryon		9	0	0	0	5	+1
D	24	Block, Ken		9	0	2	2	6	+4
D	4	Clackson, Kim			0	1	1	24	+2
G	31	Dion, Michel		4	0	0	0	0	
RW	20	Harbaruk, Nick		6	1	1	2	0	-1
C	7	Harris, Hugh		2	0	0	0	0	-1
G	30	Hoganson, Paul	< Cin	5	0	0	0	0	
D	10	Inkpen, Dave	< Cin	9	0	2	2	8	-4
C	15	Karlander, Al		6	2	1	3	0	0
RW	8	LeClerc, Rene		9	1	1	2	4	-7
RW	25	Lomenda, Mark		9	3	1	4	17	-3
RW	14	MacDonald, Blair		9	7	8	15	4	+11
D	2	Maggs, Darryl		9	1	4	5	4	-3
RW	11	McDonald, Brian		9	3	4	7	33	-5
RW	6	Paiement, Rosaire	< NE	9	0	5	5	15	-3
C	16	Parizeau, Michel		8	3	6	9	8	+7
LW	22	Peacosh, Gene	< Edm	9	3	3	6	2	-2
LW	19	Rochon, Francois		5	0	1	1	0	-1
C	17	Sicinski, Bob		9	0	3	3	4	-5
D	12	Stapleton, Pat		9	2	6	8	0	-1
LW	9	Thomas, Reg		9	7	9	16	4	+8

1976-77 Playoff Goaltending

	gp	min	ga	en	sho	w	l	gaa
Dion, Michel	4	245	17	0	0	2	2	4.16
Hoganson, Paul < Cin	5	348	17	0	1	3	2	2.93
TEAM TOTALS	9	593	34	0	1	5	4	3.44

Playoff Scores 1975-76

New England vs. Indianapolis

Apr 16	New England 4 at Indianapolis 1
Apr 17	New England 0 at Indianapolis 4
Apr 21	Indianapolis 0 at New England 3
Apr 23	Indianapolis 1 at New England 2
Apr 24	New England 0 at Indianapolis 4
Apr 27	Indianapolis 5 at New England 3
Apr 29	New England 6 at Indianapolis 0

	w	l	gf	ga
New England	4	3	19	15
Indianapolis	3	4	15	19

Playoff Scores 1976-77

Cincinnati vs. Indianapolis

Apr 9	Indianapolis 4 at Cincinnati 3 **(3 ot)***
Apr 12	Indianapolis 7 at Cincinnati 2
Apr 14	Cincinnati 3 at Indianapolis 5
Apr 16	Cincinnati 1 at Indianapolis 3

	w	l	gf	ga
Indianapolis	4	0	19	9
Cincinnati	0	4	9	19

* longest game in WHA history

Québec vs. Indianapolis

Apr 23	Indianapolis 1 at Québec 3
Apr 25	Indianapolis 3 at Québec 8
Apr 28	Québec 6 at Indianapolis 5 **(ot)**
Apr 30	Québec 0 at Indianapolis 2
May 2	Indianapolis 3 at Québec 8

	w	l	gf	ga
Québec	4	1	25	14
Indianapolis	1	4	14	25

Wayne Gretzky Racers 1978-79 Pre-Season Statistics (Indy W2, L3, T1)

gp	g	a	pts	pim
6	5	4	9	0

(points led all Racers players)

Wayne Gretzky Racers 1978-79 Regular Season Scoring Statistics

Game #	Date	Opponent	Details
1	Oct 14	Winnipeg	No scoring
2	Oct 15	Birmingham	No scoring
3	Oct 18	Québec	Assisted on Richie Leduc's 2nd period goal at 16:14 Kevin Morrison also assisted
4	Oct 20	Edmonton	Scored at 6:07 and 6:41 of the 2nd period against Dave Dryden; Morrison assisted on his first goal, while Peter Driscoll and Don Larway assisted on his second goal
5	Oct 22	New England	Assisted on Driscoll's goal at 16:56 of the 1st period; scored at 3:30 of the 3rd period, with assists to Larway and Al McLeod
6	Oct 27	Birmingham	Assisted on Larway's goal at 18:49 of the 1st period; Gerry Leroux also assisted
7, 8	Oct 28, 29	Winnipeg	No scoring

RACERS FRANCHISE PLAYER TRANSACTIONS

1974-75

Ed Dyck signed to contract, Apr 1974 • Steve Richardson signed to contract, Jun 1974 • Nick Harbaruk acquired from New England, Jun 1974 • Steve Andrascik on loan to Indianapolis by Cincinnati for 1974-75 season, Jul 1974 • Andy Brown signed to contract, Jul 1974 • Kerry Bond purchased from San Diego (WHL), Oct 1974 • Steve Andrascik and Steve Richardson traded to Michigan for Jacques Locas and Brian McDonald, Nov 1974 • Gary Bredin traded to Michigan for Bill Horton, Nov 1974 • Joe Robertson traded to Minnesota for Jim Johnson, Nov 1974 • Dick Proceviat acquired from Chicago for future considerations, Dec 1974 • Bob Woytowich purchased from Winnipeg, Dec 1974 • Murray Kennett traded to Edmonton for Ron Buchanan, Jan 1975 • Jim Hargreaves traded to San Diego for Ken Block, Jan 1975 • Murray Heatley acquired from Minnesota for future considerations, Feb 1975 • Joe Hardy traded to San Diego for future considerations (Ted Scharf), Mar 1975

1975-76

Jim Park signed to contract, Oct 1974 • Leif Holmquist signed to contract, Jun 1975 • Rights to Randy Wyrozub acquired from Edmonton, Jul 1975 • Brian Coates acquired from Denver for future considerations, Sep 1975 • Randy Wyrozub signed to contract, Sep 1975 • Blair MacDonald acquired from Edmonton for draft picks, Dec 1975 • Bill Prentice traded to Québec for Rene LeClerc, Jan 1976 • Bob Fitchner and Michel Dubois traded to Québec for Michel Parizeau, Feb 1976 • Bryon Baltimore, Mark Lomenda, Gary MacGregor and Darryl Maggs purchased from Ottawa, Jan 1976 • Dave Keon signed as free agent from defunct Minnesota, Mar 1976

1976-77

Bryan Campbell acquired from Cincinnati for future considerations, Jun 1976 • Gary MacGregor acquired from Minnesota for Dave Keon, Sep 1976 • Bryan Campbell traded to Edmonton for Gene Peacosh, Nov 1976 • Gary MacGregor traded to New England for Rosaire Paiement, Nov 1976 • Paul Hoganson and Dave Inkpen purchased from Cincinnati, Feb 1977

1977-78

Lynn Powis signed to contract, May 1977 • Kevin Morrison signed to contract, Jul 1977 • Mike Zuke and Dave Inkpen traded to Edmonton for Kevin Devine, Barry Wilkins, Rusty Patenaude and Claude St. Sauveur, Sep 1977 • Dave Fortier, Gary Inness, Pete McDuffe, Frank Spring signed to contracts, Sep 1977 • Dave Inkpen and Peter Driscoll purchased from Québec, Dec 1977 • Lynn Powis released, signed by Winnipeg, Dec 1977 • Bill Goldsworthy acquired from NY Rangers (NHL) for Frank Spring, Dec 1977 • Bryon Baltimore and Hugh Harris traded to Cincinnati for Gilles Marotte and Blaine Stoughton, Jan 1978 • Darryl Maggs and Reg Thomas traded to Cincinnati for Rich Leduc and Claude Larose, Feb 1978 • Ed Mio purchased from Birmingham, Feb 1978 • Glenn Irwin acquired from Houston for future considerations, Mar 1978 • Charles Constantin acquired from Québec for future considerations, Mar 1978 • Dale Smedsmo signed to contract, Mar 1978

1978-79

Wayne Gretzky signed to personal services contract with Indianapolis owner Nelson Skalbania, Jun 1978 • John Hughes purchased from Houston via Winnipeg, Jul 1978 • Gary Smith signed to contract, Sep 1978 • Angelo Moretto signed to contract, Sep 1978, released Nov 1978 • Bruce Greig signed to contract, Oct 1978 • Wayne Gretzky, Ed Mio and Peter Driscoll sold to Edmonton, Nov 1978 • Don Burgess bought out and released, Nov 1978 • Bryon Baltimore sold to Cincinnati, Nov 1978 • Rich Leduc, Kevin Morrison sold to Québec, Nov 1978 • Wes George acquired from Edmonton in Nov 1978 • Dean Magee, Mark Messier signed to contracts, Nov 1978 • Remainder declared free agents after team folds, Dec 1978

THE BLOOD OF GILLES MAROTTE

Author Timothy Gassen wrote the following 2008 feature piece for InsideHockey Magazine after the publication of the first edition of this book.

My head knows that it is just a piece of cloth. But my heart knows that a hockey jersey is also the place where the game itself lives. It is where hockey players spend those brief minutes that nature, talent and hard work allow them to play the game I love. So finding, holding, perhaps even owning an original 1970s World Hockey Association game jersey for my hometown major league Indianapolis Racers had been a holy grail for me, for decades now.

A few days ago, I finally held one, and I let the royal blue polyester slide over my hands. I reveled at the obvious damage it had endured: black marks from stick blades and puck hits over the Racers crest, and snags and burns from collisions at such speed and force that the polyester literally melted in spots. There were holes, fabric runs and damage that comes only from a hockey player giving his sweat and his tears for his teammates.

And then I saw the blood of Gilles Marotte. He must have taken a blow to the face, because the trail of blood starts at the top of the jersey, just under the collar. It continues through the elegant Racers logo crest, and finishes at the bottom waist hem. Neither the team's equipment manager nor time itself could mitigate the stains. They're just faded brown spots now, but this piece of cloth, this Racers' game jersey, this childhood dream of mine, would always carry with it a bit of Gilles Marotte.

A rugged NHL and WHA veteran for almost 900 games in 13 seasons from 1965-1978, defenseman Gilles Marotte will never again wear his final major league jersey – he died of pancreatic cancer in 2005 at age 60. The irony for me is that Gilles was never one of my favorite Racers as I followed the club like a religious cult in the late 1970s. He only played the last half of the 1977-78 season with Indy, the last stop of his long, tiring career. While I can still remember details of many Racers as they hopped over the bench onto the ice decades ago, Gilles Marotte is only a hazy memory for me.

But his legacy was handed to me, along with his last jersey, at the 2007 reunion of players and fans brought together by the publication of the first edition of my Racers book. One of the Racers Booster Club officers had kept the jersey safe and sound through the decades, and brought it to me after hearing of my pleas to somehow own one. It is no exaggeration of any kind to say that I stopped breathing and turned absolute white when it was given to me. No one ever expects to actually hold the grail they seek.

Matter-of-fact, quiet and full of true Midwest humility, my new Racers Booster friend wanted to believe this was no big deal, no giant favor, nothing but the act of giving an old jersey to a younger fan. But deep down, in her eyes, it seemed to me that she was delighted that it could bring such exhilaration. Perhaps she was delighted that the Racers, dead since 1979, perhaps would live again in this little way.

She did know, by the way, that an Indianapolis Racers jersey such as this one fetches thousands of dollars at auction. But she also knew that money couldn't buy the passion that flashed in my eyes when I saw it. It will never meet the auction block while I breath; heck, I might be wearing it when I meet up with Gilles Marotte in my hockey afterlife.

And I hope no one saw this next bit: I left the party briefly and went outside, in the autumnal Indiana sunshine, and put on the jersey. I jumped for joy like my Racers had just scored a game winning goal, like I was 13 again.

"Just a piece of cloth," I tried to believe.

And once I saw the blood – this player's sacrifice – on the jersey, I had to know more about Gilles Marotte. I understand that every hockey player will get blood on his jersey, and much of the time it'll be his own, too. But it made even more sense when I remembered that Gilles Marotte's nickname throughout the hockey world was "Captain Crunch." He was renowned for his hitting, his gritty style, and his solid, thick physique.

I looked down at the sleeves of this size 48 Rawlings shirt, and saw how his 200 pound, 5' 9" frame filled it like a fireplug. "Captain Crunch" was all about contact, and so I would have been surprised if his blood didn't grace his work clothes. I also wondered: even when he played in the 1973 NHL All-Star game, did he hit the other team?

I'm pretty certain that this is the same blue Racers jersey Gilles wore in the official 1977-78 Racers team photo I have in this book, taken just after he joined the squad halfway through the season. The WHA has switched "home" and "away" colors for that campaign, so the beautiful blue shirts were the "home" apparel for the year. Based on the high amount of game wear, it's a good guess that the team only issued this one blue "home" jersey for half of Gilles' 44 Racers games. It even still had its name plate on the back when my Booster member obtained it from the team after the 1978 season – which is an extremely rare find for the era, and means it most likely was his last jersey.

My Racers friend attempted to give this jersey back to Gilles Marotte late in his life, but he declined. It was explained that he didn't want to relive the end of his career, from a hard, difficult year.

So a final irony is clear to me – the jersey Gilles Marotte didn't want to wear again will now assure that his memory will remain alive with hockey fans. He now holds a special place for me on my childhood team that will always be my favorite. So I'll wear this simple piece of cloth at every hockey game I can, and when asked the inevitable "Weren't the Racers Wayne Gretzky's first team?" I'll instead explain all about "Captain Crunch" – and the blood of Gilles Marotte.

Gilles "Captain Crunch" Marotte in 1978 action with his now-treasured Racers jersey.

Indianapolis goaltender **Andy Brown** at the **Minnesota Fighting Saints** in 1975. Notice an important detail: Brown is watching the puck zoom past him without wearing a mask. He was the last major league goaltender to play mask-less, though he wore one during practice with the Racers. (*Enhanced team photo*)

Robbie Ftorek and **Dennis Sobchuk** of the **Phoenix Roadrunners** screen Racers goalie **Andy Brown** during the 1974-1975 season. Brown battled valiantly in goal throughout the Racers' difficult first year.

In battle with the WHA champion **Houston Aeros**, circa 1976. (*Previously unpublished team photo*)

Pat Stapleton and goaltender **Andy Brown** defend against Houston's **Gordon Labossiere**, circa 1976. *(Previously unpublished team photo)*

Andy Brown pushes a **Cleveland Crusader** out of the way (above), while **Ed Dyck** protects his crease (left), both during the Racers' first 1974-1975 season.

(courtesy The Indianapolis Star)

Rusty Patenaude, **Claude St. Sauveur** and **Darryl Maggs** (l to r) patrol home ice early in the 1977-1978 season (above), while **John Sheridan** and **Bob Fitchner** (l to r) rush a **Vancouver Blazer** during 1974-1975. (*Previously unpublished photos*)

Racers superstar **Pat Stapleton** (far left) works with his defensive partner **Kim Clackson** (center) against the Houston Aeros' **John Tonelli** (far right) in the Houston Summit. *(Previously unpublished team photo)*

Kim Clackson moves the Houston Aeros' **Don Larway** out of the way (above). *(Previously unpublished team photo)*

A franchise promotional mailer drumming up season ticket sales for the Racers before the team's 1975-1976 season (above). Indianapolis was a notorious day-of-game walk-up ticket buying market, and the perpetual difficulty in selling season tickets dogged the Racers franchise for its entire existence. Indianapolis ironically often led the league in game attendance, but the lack of a substantial season ticket base made the team's long-term financial planning continually nebulous.

"Through these portals pass the world's best loved hockey team" read the bedsheet banner over the tunnel that the Racers used to enter and exit the ice at Market Square Arena (top). The sentiment was not mere words — many who played for the Racers contend that no other community loved their team to the utmost quite like Indianapolis. *(Previously unpublished photo)*

The Racers Booster Club (below, circa 1975) was one of the largest in either of the major leagues, and was renowned for its devotion. This dedication made it difficult for the minor league teams in Indianapolis in the 1980s and 1990s to take firm hold of the market. Indy had been to the major leagues, and after the devotion to the Racers it was difficult for many to accept a demotion to the minors.

Game programs during the 1977-78 season featured paintings by illustrator **Steve Fox** that were based on player photographs (above and on opposite page). These original paintings used for publication remain unique and prized team mementos. Racers programs in general were among the best and most visually interesting from WHA teams.

Veteran goaltender **Gary Inness** (above) poses without his usual game mask.

Rosaire Paiement (top left), **Michel Parizeau** (top right), **Rusty Patenaude** (bottom left) and **Kevin Morrison** (bottom right) in more of **Steve Fox**'s 1977-78 Racers game program cover paintings.

Racers game progam covers, 1974-1978 (this page and opposite). **Ron Buchanan** is pictured top left and **Bob Sicinski** top right from the team's first season in 1974-1975.

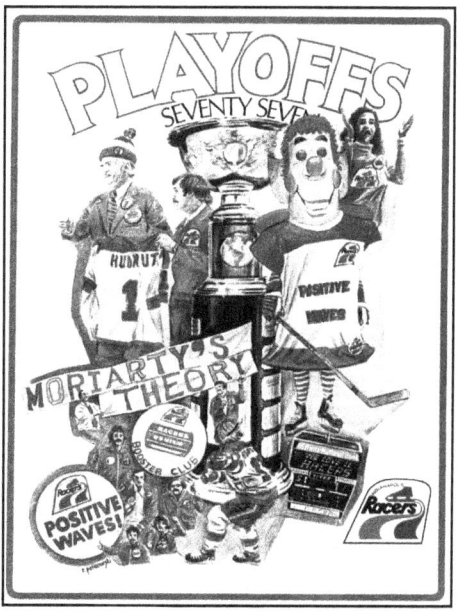

Racers mascot **Moriarty, The AVCO World Trophy** and the popular **"Positive Waves"** fan campaign all adorned the team's 1977 playoff program (above right), while **Wayne Gretzky** (lower right) was featured on his only WHA Racers game progam cover in Fall 1978.

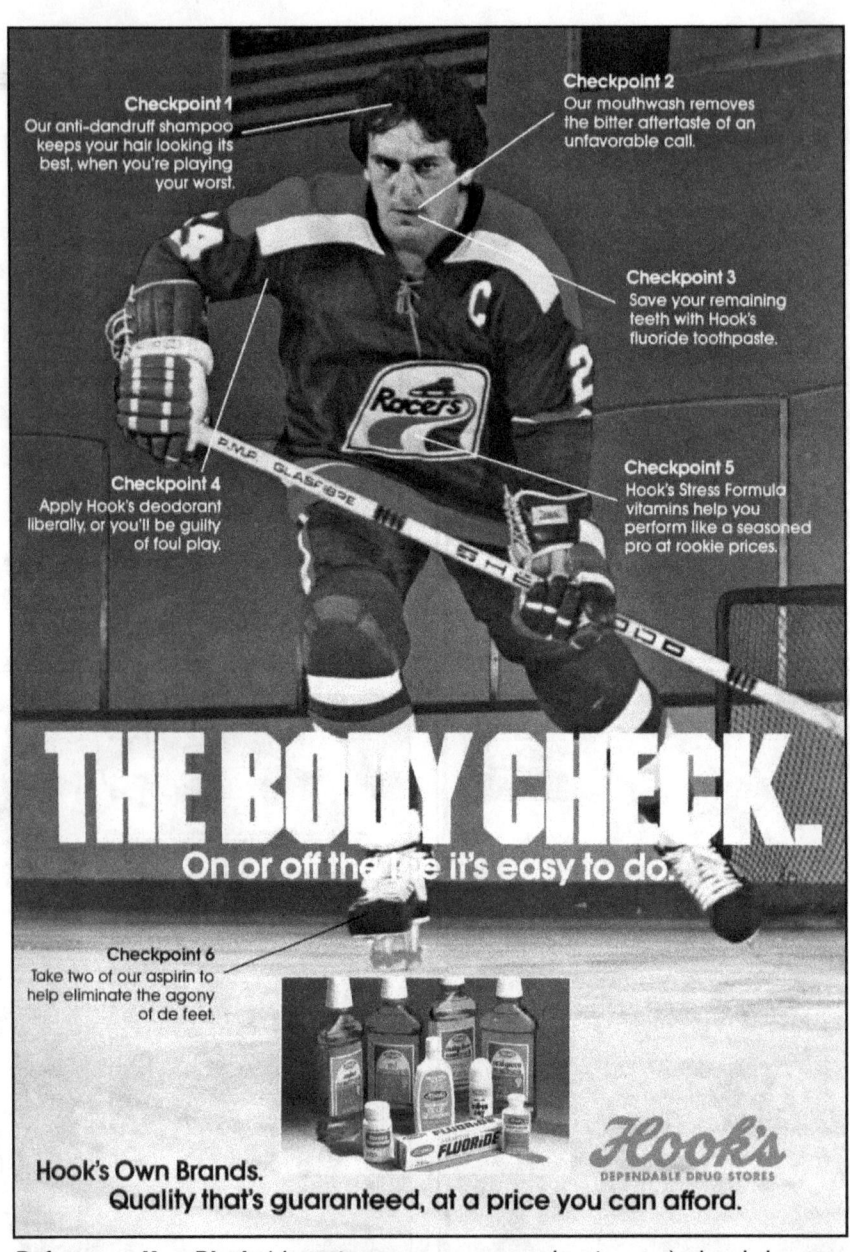

Defenseman **Ken Block** (above in a game program advertisement) played the most games of any player in Racers history (267), and was a longtime Captain of the team. His steady solid play and team-first professionalism was a bedrock for the franchise through all of its upheaval, and he was one of the few players to see the franchise from its humble beginnings and rise to respectability through its heart-wrenching demise in late 1978.

Ken Block, a dependable Captain remembered and admired by Indianapolis hockey fans for his grit and durability. Block's jersey shows the marks of battle he endured during his four-plus years in Indianapolis. Talented journeymen players such as Block found success and acceptance in the WHA — and proved they were major leaguers. *(Previously unpublished photo)*

TUESDAY, JUNE 13, 1978 — THE INDIANAPOLIS STAR — PAGE 21

17-YEAR-OLD POSSIBLY 'BEST PLAYER IN WORLD'

Racers Get Top Canadian Junior

By JOHN BANSCH
Assistant Sports Editor

Nelson Skalbania has scored a major triumph in his battle to become a leading figure in the world of professional hockey.

The wealthy owner of the Indianapolis Racers made his move Monday by announcing the signing of 17-year-old Wayne Gretzky to a seven-year personal services contract estimated to be worth around $2 million.

Considered the finest junior skater to emerge from Canada since Bobby Orr and said to have the same potential as Gordie Howe and Bobby Hull, the youthful centerman is ticketed to perform with the Racers in the upcoming World Hockey Association season.

Unless there are complications which prohibit Gretzky from playing here, he will be the highest-paid player in the league, according to Skalbania.

LAST WINTER he scored 70 goals and 112 assists as a member of the Sault Ste. Marie Greyhounds in the Ontario Hockey Association. He then went on to lead all scorers in world tournament play, which included teams from Russia, Czechoslovakia, Sweden and Finland.

Skalbania termed Gretzky the world's best junior center and possibly the "best player in the world." Gus Badali, the Toronto-based agent who negotiated the transaction, observed, "Wayne has unbelievable puck sense, he mesmerizes the opposition, and he predicted the poorest player on the Racers will score 30 goals if he's on Gretzky's line."

The signing was announced at about the time the rival National Hockey League opened its summer meetings at Montreal. It is expected the signing will be an issue in a statement against the signing since in effect it bars a rule which prohibits teams from signing juniors until they reach 20 years of age.

Skalbania could care less.

"WE HAVE BEEN raped," he said in reference to WHA players who have jumped to the NHL. Included among those who have changed leagues are Anders Hedberg and Ulf Nilsson, two former Winnipeg stars now with the New York Rangers. "If we expect to maintain the caliber of play we have had in the WHA, we can only resort to raiding the underage juniors."

There have been reports the NHL will "invite" Edmonton, Quebec, New England and Winnipeg to join the older league next winter. Skalbania's latest move could force Indianapolis to be considered.

Asked about the situation, the Racers owner was vague. He did say "the clout of the signing makes the clout on our part." However, he would not say any talk because Indianapolis was not mentioned in reports of possible new NHL teams.

The signing will also be the subject of much discussion throughout Canada, according to Badali. "This may O.J. Simpson with impact as the signing did in the United States."

SKALBANIA SAID the acquisition of Gretzky "precludes my going to Houston." It had been rumored that Skalbania would attempt to purchase the financially distressed Houston franchise and possibly move it to the NHL. "Right now no changes are contemplated in the Racers situation," he added.

Gretzky, a long-haired blond who somewhat resembles tennis star Vitas Gerulaitis, said he is "very excited" about playing for the Racers.

"This is a very big challenge," said the slender skater, who said his 5-11, 155-pound frame may be his "biggest downfall."

The newest Racer admitted he "may be a little small for professional hockey, but the 'good runs' at the opposition 'taking off' on him in the WHA like they did in Canada.

Gretzky has been labeled a "slow" skater. Badali says that's not true. "Wayne is very fluid and at times it just appears he's slow," asserted the agent.

A NATIVE of Brantford, Ont., Gretzky began skating when he was 2 years old. When he was 8 he was carrying being touted as the next great Canadian superstar. At 11 he scored 378 goals in 68 games. He was a legend before he was a teen-ager.

Gretzky still has one year of high school to finish. Racers officials will seek to enroll him in summer school when he returns to Indianapolis in a couple of weeks.

Pressed as to the status of naming a coach, he said the search is "narrowing down." Is Jacques Demers, former Racer coach among the candidates? "No comment," was the reply. When will a coach be named? "Soon," Skalbania said.

TOP JUNIOR PROSPECT — Wayne Gretzky, considered the finest junior skater to come out of Canadian junior hockey since Bobby Orr, adjusts his tie as he is introduced to the news media Monday at the Columbia Club by Indianapolis Racers owner Nelson Skalbania. The 17-year-old center was signed by Skalbania to a seven-year personal services contract and is expected to give the Racers more scoring punch. He scored 70 goals and added 112 assists last year with the Sault Ste. Marie Greyhounds of the Ontario Hockey Association. (UPI Photo)

Hope filled the hearts of Racers fans with the announcement in the summer of 1978 that teenage phenomenom **Wayne Gretzky** would play his first major league season in Indianapolis. Only later would it become known that Gretzky's move to Edmonton was part of an intricate chess game to ensure the merger of the WHA and rival NHL — and that the Racers would be cast aside in the process. (courtesy The Indianapolis Star)

The summer 1978 Indianapolis newspaper ad for the Great Gretzky Fan Club (above), and a snapshot of **Wayne Gretzky** (top right) at one of the listed department store personal appearances. His first major league training camp with the WHA Indianapolis Racers was only days away. *(ad courtesy The Indianapolis Star)*

All-Star **Pat "Whitey" Stapleton** (left) is reunited with another Racers favorite **Kim Clackson** (right) at the **2010 WHA Hall of Fame** game in Cleveland, Ohio. Stapleton brought stability and credibility to the Racers in 1975 and he mentored then-rookie Clackson as his defensive partner. The cool and calm demeanor of Stapleton's play contrasted vividly with Clackson's tough and rough physical style, and the effective combination helped guide the Racers to the 1975-76 WHA Eastern Division championship. Stapleton was inducted into the WHA Hall of Fame in 2010, and is rightfully remembered as one of the finest defensive players in the history of major league hockey. (*WHA Hall of Fame photo*)

ACKNOWLEDGEMENTS

Special thanks to Sarah Gassen for her editorial contributions. Sarah is an award-winning reporter and editorial writer at the author's former newspaper, the Arizona Daily Star.

Thanks also to Scott Adam Surgent for entertaining my questions about the Racers franchise and for providing important team materials and statistics, and Barry Dunlop, who discussed and generously shared his extensive WHA collection of memorabilia. A hearty thanks also to Bruce Boggess, who generously contributed important graphic materials and information. Sandy Booth, Michael McDonald, Mike Fasig, Dave Phelan, David Weiser and Jamie Burrell graciously provided other memorabilia and photos. Judy Stuart contributed essential photos and firsthand information, Ralph Slate contributed the all-time Racers player roster, and Curtis Walker kindly shared many items from his WHA newspaper archives. The help and assistance of Ted Green and The Indianapolis Star is also greatly appreciated. Finally, Tom Doherty helped with publishing details, and Ed Bertschy was instrumental with the first edition book layout.

Thank you all!

SOURCE ATTRIBUTIONS

As explained in the Preface, factual information and quotes which are included without attribution are from firsthand reporting and interviews the author conducted personally. Other factual sources, including newspapers, magazines and books are attributed specifically in the text or photographic captions. Statistics are cited from WHA league and team sources.

BOOK SOURCES

"Gretzky," by Walter Gretzky and Jim Taylor, 1984, Avon Books, Canada
"Same Game, Different Name," by Jack Lautier and Frank Polnasnek, 1996,
    Glacier Publishing, USA
"Big Pucks & Blue Pucks," by Murray Greig, 1997, Macmillan Books, Canada
"Messier," by Jeff Z. Klein, 2003, Triumph Books, USA
"The Complete Historical and Statistical Reference to the World Hockey
    Association," (7th Edition) by Scott Adam Surgent, 2004, USA
"The Rebel League," by Ed Willes, 2004, McClelland & Stewart, Ltd., Canada

PHOTO CREDITS

Thank you to The Indianapolis Star for its kind permission to use their photo archives. Photographs also include Racers and WHA league promo items. Most official team promotional photos did not include a specific photographer's credit, but we do know the names of some of the talented photographers who captured the Racers. They include: Chuck Fandrei, Donna Fandrei, Steve Fox, Robert Britt, Don Blake, Jerry Ganter, Bud Jones, Ron McQueeney, Ed Moss, Mary Ann Carter, Steve Snoddy and Glenn Binegar.

Some included materials are believed to be in the public domain or are shown within fair use guidelines. Trademarks remain the property of their owners and are shown for historical purposes. Efforts have been made to trace the origin of materials; please contact the author if you are the verifiable current copyright owner of any material. Thank you to all the talented photographers and media members who covered the WHA Racers from 1974-1979.

ABOUT THE AUTHOR

Timothy Gassen is president of the World Hockey Association Hall of Fame, and an acknowledged expert on the history of the WHA. He has written, produced and directed the more than 12 hours of WHA video documentaries that are available as the multi-disc WHA Hall of Fame DVD and Blu-ray Disc series. Included in that series is a volume detailing the Racers titled "Gretzky, Indy & The WHA."

His other book on the World Hockey Association, "The WHA Hall of Fame: A Photographic History Of The Rebel League 1972-1979" is published by St. Johann Press. It features many more previously unpublished Indianapolis Racers photos.

Gassen has worked professionally as a journalist and filmmaker since 1979. In 1995 and 2017 he won an Arizona Press Club Award for his hockey coverage, and he's served as a college hockey team media director, college and pro hockey radio man, and TV broadcaster. He has also been a longtime columnist for InsideHockey Magazine and the Arizona Daily Star newspaper, and this is his fourth book.

Visit the author's company Web site at **www.purple-cactus.tv** and the WHA Hall of Fame at both **WHAhof.com** and **whaRACERS.com**

INDEX

A
All-Star Game (WHA) 1974-75: 10
All-Star Game (WHA) 1976: 13
All-Star Game (WHA) 1977: 30, 33, 93-94, 114 (photo)
All-Star Game (WHA) 1978: 36
Allen, Kevin: 26
American Basketball Association: 8, 28, 73, 93
American Hockey League: 93
Anderson, Glenn: 103
Ash, Bob: 67
Associated Press: 46
Attendance figures: 52
AVCO Cup (AVCO World Trophy): 25, 77

B
Badali, Gus: 40
Baldwin, Howard: 25, 50, 51
Baltimore, Bryon "Balty": 14, 35, 68-69, 76-77, 80, 92, 119
Baltimore Blades: 118
Bassett, John: 38,
Beckett Hockey Card Monthly (magazine): 26, 45
Ben Hatskin Award for Best Goaltender: 23
Bernier, Serge: 77, 111
Berry, Tom: 30, 87
"Big Bucks and Blue Pucks" (book): 12, 27, 42
Birmingham Bulls: 38, 96, 98, 112
Blatchford, Christie: 25
Block, Ken: 12, 14-15, 42-44, 55, 59-60, 67-70, 73-80 (interview), 99, 108, 120, 127, 168, 169
Blumenstock, Kathy: 42
Boggess, Bruce: 17, 41, 108-110 (interview)
Bond, Kerry: 67, 68
Broad Ripple High School: 46
Broad Street Bullies: 95
Bromley, Gary: 98
Browitt, James: 67-68, 75
Brown, Andy: 8, 10, 18, 58, 61, 67, 69, 84, 95, 123, 154-155, 157-158
Buchanan, Ron: 67, 166
Buffalo Sabres (NHL): 89
Bulldog Lounge: 91
Burgess, Don: 70

C
Caldwell, David: 29
Calgary Cowboys: 44, 89, 98
Cairns, Michel: 59, 68, 69
Carey, John: 70
Carlson, Steve ("Hanson Brother"): 22
Carroll, Bill: 67, 70
Channel 6 TV (Indianapolis): 37, 121
Channel 13 TV (Indianapolis): 36, 106
Chicago Blackhawks (NHL): 12, 15, 27, 92
Chicago Cougars: 15
Chipperfield, Ron: 103
Cincinnati Stingers: 20, 30-36, 44, 49, 53, 77-78, 91-92, 99, 103, 108, 111-112, 119
Clackson, Kim "Clacker": 12-13, 31, 59, 61, 68-69, 76, 80, 83, 121, 161, 166, 172
Cleveland Crusaders: 108, 158
Cloutier, Real: 77, 111
Coates, Brian: 68
Coffey, Paul: 103
Columbus Blue Jackets (NHL): 56
Conacher, Brian: 69, 87
Constantin, Charles: 70
Coppock, Chet: 50
Czechoslovakia national team: 30, 59

D
Dellapina, John: 48
Demers, Jacques: 10-14, 20, 23, 26, 28, 30, 33-35, 45, 53, 59, 68-69, 75-77, 80, 82, 90-92, 108-109, 112-113, 120, 122
Deneau, Paul: 11, 30
Denny, Dick: 23, 89, 90
Denver Spurs: 118
Desjardine, Ken: 67
Detroit Red Wings (NHL): 81
Devine, Kevin: 70
Dion, Michel: 18, 23, 33, 63, 68-69, 77-78, 92, 95-96, 120-121, 125
Driscoll, Peter: 46, 70, 100
Dryden, Dave: 45
Ducote, Harold: 30
Dyck, Ed: 8, 67, 158

E
Eastern Division (WHA): 20, 21, 30
Eastern Division Champions Portrait (1975-76): 68
Edmonton Oilers (WHA): 27, 39, 41, 46-47, 49, 51, 54, 74, 86, 99-101, 115, 170
Edmonton Oilers (NHL): 49, 54, 103
Edmonton Journal (newspaper): 48
Edmonton Sun (newspaper): 39, 45, 54
Ego, Ron: 106
ESPN (television): 20
European, players and style of play: 24, 30, 54, 102
Exhibition games, WHA vs. NHL: 24, 25, 44

F
Fitchner, Bob: 67, 159

Fortier, Dave: 70
Fotiou, Nick: 13
Fox, Steve: 164
Francis, Emile: 44
Free agent contracts: 27
French Canadian players: 16
French, John: 70
Friday, Bill: 31
Ftorek, Robbie: 155
Fuson, Wayne: 21

G

Garrett, John: 98
Gassen, Timothy: 72, 121 (photos)
Givens, David: 34
Gleeson, Fraser: 67
Goldsworthy, Bill: 35, 70, 80, 99-101, 106, 122, 126
Goldthorpe, Billy: 118
Goulet, Michel: 28
Greb, Randy: 9, 50, 11-112 (interview)
Greig, Murray: 12, 27, 42
"Gretzky" (book): 39, 43
Gretzky, Walter: 39, 43
Gretzky, Wayne ("The Great One"): 26-28, 37-47, 50-55, 64-65, 71, 79-80, 86-87, 96, 99-100, 103, 107, 110, 112, 127-128, 167, 170-171
Griffin, Tom: 34

H

Harbaruk, Nick: 8, 67, 68, 123
Hardy, Joe: 67
Harris, Hugh: 13-14, 24, 29-31, 35, 55-56, 58, 68-69, 78, 82, 89-94 (interview), 114, 121
Hedberg, Anders: 24
Hockey Digest, the: 23
Hockey Management, Inc.: 30
Hockey News, the: 6, 40-41, 43-44
Hoganson, Paul "Hoagie": 96, 119, 125
Holmquist, Leif: 68
Horton, Bill: 67
Houston Aeros: 7, 11, 36, 39-40, 51, 156, 157, 161
Howe, Gordie ("Mr. Hockey"): 7, 17, 93-94, 106, 108, 117
Howe, Mark: 7
Howe, Marty: 7
Hull, Bobby: 17, 24, 45, 93-94, 108
Humphreys, Nat: 19
Hunter, Douglas: 42

I

Indiana National Bank: 33-34
Indiana Professional Sports Management: 7

Indianapolis: 8, 28, 32, 46-47, 51-55, 87, 93
Indianapolis Checkers (team): 56, 97, 107, 112
Indianapolis Colts football: 19
Indianapolis Hockey Ltd.: 30
Indianapolis Ice (team): 107, 112
Indianapolis News, the: 21, 23, 28, 34, 53, 89
Indianapolis Pacers basketball: 8, 19, 28, 38, 52, 93
Indianapolis Racers: 7, 9, 14, 20-22, 28, 31-35, 37, 39-40, 41-46, 48-54, 56, 80, 83, 87, 92, 97, 123
Indianapolis Racers Booster Club: 28-29, 34, 54-55, 61, 109, 120, 151, 163
Indianapolis Star, the: 22, 30, 34, 89
Ingram, Ron: 35, 78, 85, 92, 96, 99, 122, 126
Inkpen, Dave: 70
Inness, Gary "Inch": 43-44, 58, 61, 70, 96, 98, 99, 164
InsideHockey magazine: 151
Internal Revenue Service: 51
International Hockey League: 97
Irwin, Glen: 70

J

Jersey Knights: 74
Johnson, Jim: 67
Johnston, Robert: 46
Jones, Terry: 39, 45

K

Karlander, Al: 12-13, 18-19, 43-44, 51, 61, 68-69, 81-88 (interview)
"Kelly's Heroes" (movie): 13, 29
Keon, Dave: 21, 68, 108, 116, 124

L

Lafleur, Guy: 16
Lamey, "Hockey Bob": 18-19, 37, 55, 111, 116
Larose, Claude: 54, 70, 111
Larose, France: 54
Larway, Don: 44
Lautier, Jack: 26, 51
LeClerc, Renald: 16, 62, 68-70, 99, 127
Leduc, Rich: 48, 70, 92
LeRose, Don: 70, 80
Libby, Bill: 6
Liebengood, Pete: 36, 37, 106
Liut, Mike: 92
Lomenda, Mark: 68, 69
Lowe, Kevin: 103

M

MacDonald, Blair (BJ): 30, 61, 68-69, 114, 116
Mackin, Bob: 41

Maggs, Darryl: 33, 35, 68-69, 76-77, 117, 159
Mahovlich, Frank: 10, 108
Maple Leaf Gardens: 21
Marlow, Walt: 29
Market Square Arena: 9, 15, 21, 28-29, 32, 36, 44, 52, 56-57, 62, 83, 93, 97, 105, 107, 109, 115, 121
Marotte, Gilles "Captain Crunch": 70, 80, 99, 151-153
Matheson, Jim: 48
McDonald, Brian: 32-33, 67-69, 91, 117, 121
McDuffe, Peter: 96
McLeod, Don "Smokey": 98
McNab, Max: 25
Melrose, Barry: 20
Merger (WHA and NHL): 25, 27, 34, 37-39, 41-42, 51, 53-55, 65, 79, 86, 100, 115, 170
Messier, Doug: 48, 49
Messier, Mark ("Moose"): 27-28, 48-49, 54-56, 64, 66, 79, 103, 112
"Messier" (book): 40, 49
Michigan Stags: 9,
Minnesota Fighting Saints: 9, 25
Mio, Ed: 26, 35, 41, 46-47, 70, 96, 98-104 (interview)
Mohawk Valley Comets: 14, 95
Montreal Canadiens (NHL): 11, 24, 44, 91
Montreal Forum: 56
Moore, Gerry: 8, 10-11, 35, 67, 75-76, 122
Moriarity / Moriarty (Racers mascot): 29, 121, 167
Morrison, Kevin: 70, 165
Moss, Doug: 48

N

National Basketball Association: 8, 28, 56, 73
National Football League: 56
National Hockey League: 8, 24, 26, 39, 46, 54, 80
Neale, Harry: 25
Negative Waves: 90
New England Whalers: 13, 21-22, 27, 36, 39, 53-54, 77, 81-82, 84, 91, 118
New York Daily News: 48, 49
New York Golden Blades: 74
New York Islanders (NHL): 97
New York Raiders: 73-75
Nielson company (sports cards): 65
North Central High School: 36, 121
Nilsson, Kent: 28
Nilsson, Ulf: 24
North American Hockey League: 14, 95
Northern Lights, the (newspaper): 37

O

O'Connor, Larry: 34
Ogilthorpe, Ogie (movie character): 118

O-Pee-Chee (sports cards): 58
Overpeck, Dave: 22-23, 30, 89, 90

P

Pacific Hockey League: 97
Paiement, Rosaire: 59, 69-70, 126, 165
Parizeau, Michel: 30, 59, 68-70, 90, 114, 127, 165
Park, Jim: 14, 21, 35, 60, 68-70, 95-97 (interview), 98-99, 117, 125, 167
Patenaude, Rusty: 36, 70, 159, 165
Peacosh, Gene: 31, 55, 61, 69, 111, 120
Pelkowski, Robert: 63
Philadelphia Flyers (NHL): 44, 95
Phoenix Coyotes (NHL): 47-48, 101, 103
Phoenix Roadrunners: 21, 155
Pickering, Billy: 15-18, 22, 31-32, 54, 72 (photo), 105
Pickering, Dave: 15-16, 18, 22, 31-32, 36, 38, 54, 56, 72 (photo), 105-107 (interview)
Plager, Barclay: 44
Plante, Jacques: 37, 108
Pocklington, Peter: 51, 74
Polnasnek, Frank: 26, 51
Positive Waves: 13-14, 29, 32, 55, 89-91, 93, 167
Prentice, Bill: 70,
Proceviat, Dick: 59, 67-69, 77, 115, 118

Q

Québec Nordiques: 25, 27, 30, 32, 45, 49, 54, 77, 96, 111

R

Rafter Rats, the: 15, 105
"Rebel League" (book): 47
Reserve clause: 27
Riverfront Coliseum (Cincinnati): 30
Roberts, Craig: 37, 121
Roberts, Gordie: 91
Robson, Gordon: 51
Rochon, Francois: 68-69
Rosen, Harvey: 35
Rule changes: 27, 102

S

"Same Game, Different Name" (book): 26, 44, 51
Sault Ste. Marie Greyhounds: 40, 42
St. Albert Saints: 48, 49
St. Louis Blues (NHL): 44, 90
St. Sauveur, Claude: 70, 80, 159
San Diego Mariners: 118
Sather, Glen: 49, 101, 103
Scharf, Ted: 13, 68, 118, 121

Season 1974-75: 67 (Racers team photo), 115, 123 (opening night roster photo), 155, 158-159, 166
Season 1975-76: 10, 13, 18, 21, 23, 77, 90, 120, 161-162
Season 1975-76 Playoffs: 14, 20-22, 57, 84, 91, 124 (playoff roster photo)
Season 1975-76 Eastern Division Champions: 68 (Racers team photo), 77, 95
Season 1976-77: 25, 30, 33, 64, 69 (Racers team photo), 77, 84, 91-92, 95, 120
Season 1976-77 Playoffs: 31, 95, 119, 125 (playoff roster photo), 167
Season 1977-78: 30, 33, 52, 62, 70 (Racers team photo), 78, 96, 98, 112, 126 (late season roster photo), 152, 159, 164-165
Season 1978-79: 38, 51-52, 66, 71 (Racers team photo), 78, 86, 99-100, 107, 122, 127 (early season roster photo), 167
Shaver, Judy: 36
Sheridan, John: 58, 67, 159
Sicinkski, Bob: 67-69, 123, 166
Skalbania, Nelson: 34-46, 48-53, 74, 78, 86-87, 96, 108, 110, 122, 126
"Slapshot" (movie): 95, 118
Smedsmo, Dale: 28-29
Smith, Gary: 50, 99
Sobchuk, Dennis: 30, 155
Sports Illustrated (magazine): 42, 53
Stanley Cup: 11, 27, 49, 54, 91, 103
Stapleton, Pat "Whitey" ("The General"): 12, 14, 30, 33, 42-43, 45-46, 48-50, 55, 68-69, 76-77, 83, 85-86, 90, 92, 99, 110, 113-114, 118, 122, 157, 160, 167, 172
Stoughton, Blaine: 48, 70, 92, 99
Stuart, Judy: 28, 54-55
SuperFans: 15-18, 22, 29, 31-32, 36, 45, 54-56, 72 (photo), 105, 107, 121
Surgent, Scott Adam: 39
Swiss, Eddie: 68-69, 109

T

Tardif, Marc: 77
"The Complete Historical and Statistical Reference to the WHA" (book): 39
"The Glory Barons" (book): 42
"The Rebel League" (book): 27, 40, 51
Thomas, Reg: 35, 55, 68-69, 80, 111, 118, 166
Toronto Globe & Mail (newspaper): 10, 25, 34-35, 40-41, 46, 50-51
Toronto Maple Leafs (NHL): 21
Toronto Toros: 10, 21, 95
Tremblay, J.C.: 77

V

Vancouver Blazers: 159
Vancouver Courier (newspaper): 41
Vass, George: 23

W

Waddell, Alex: 37
Wahle, Don: 120
Washington Capitals (NHL): 25, 117
Weissert, John: 7
Western Hockey League: 49
WHA Hall of Fame: 172
Whitlock, Bob: 12, 67
WIBC (Indianapolis radio): 19, 116
Wides, Barry: 68-69, 80
Wilkins, Barry: 70
Willes, Ed: 27, 40, 51
Wilson-Davis Advertising Agency: 8
Winnipeg Jets (WHA): 24, 26-27, 36, 45, 49, 54
Winnipeg Jets (NHL): 54
Winnipeg "Jet Stream" magazine: 35
Wirtz, William: 27
Wiste, Jim: 67
Wood, Wayne: 98
World Hockey Association: 8, 19, 24, 26-27, 40, 51-54, 73, 97
Woytowich, Bob: 67-68

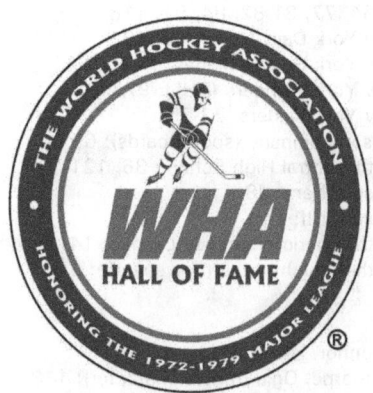

www.ingramcontent.com/pod-product-compliance
Lightning Source LLC
Chambersburg PA
CBHW061759110426
42742CB00012BB/2191